GREAT
WOMEN AUTHORS

CROSSWAY BOOKS BY
JANE STUART SMITH AND BETTY CARLSON

The Gift of Music
Great Christian Hymn Writers
Great Women Authors

GREAT

WOMEN AUTHORS

THEIR LIVES AND
THEIR LITERATURE

JANE STUART SMITH
&
BETTY CARLSON

CROSSWAY BOOKS • WHEATON, ILLINOIS
A DIVISION OF GOOD NEWS PUBLISHERS

Great Women Authors

Copyright © 1999 by Jane Stuart Smith and Betty Carlson.

Published by Crossway Books
    a division of
    Good News Publishers
    1300 Crescent Street
    Wheaton, Illinois 60187.

Scripture references marked NKJV are taken from the *New King James Version.* Copyright © 1982, Thomas Nelson, Inc. Used by permission.

Cover design and illustration: Big Picture Design

Cover photo: Tony Stone Images

First printing, 1999

Printed in the United States of America

Library of Congress Cataloging-in-Publication Data
Smith, Jane Stuart.
    Great women authors : their lives and their literature / Jane Stuart
Smith, and Betty Carlson.
        p.   cm.
    Includes bibliographical references and index.
    ISBN 1-58134-066-4 (trade pbk. : alk. paper)
    1. English literature—Women authors—History and criticism.
2. American literature—Women authors—History and criticism.
3. Women authors, American—Biography. 4. Women authors, English—
Biography. I. Carlson, Betty. II. Title.
PR111.S65 1999
820.9'9287—dc21   99-12069
                                                                CIP

15	14	13	12	11	10	09	08	07	06	05	04	03	02	01	00	99
15	14	13	12	11	10	9	8	7	6	5	4	3	2	1		

*We dedicate this book to
Peggy Hatch, always helpful,
and to Jane Kelly and Margy Watkins,
enthusiastic supporters.*

CONTENTS

INTRODUCTION

To know about the life of an author adds to the understanding and appreciation of his or her work. You will find a variety of beliefs and disbeliefs throughout these pages, but we are convinced that all the gifts of men and women are given to them by God. Talents and abilities come as a result of common grace through the influence of the Holy Spirit. The cultivation of the arts is not redemptive, but it is good, improving peoples' minds and giving them richer, more fulfilling lives.

Unfortunately people often give praise to those who have created works of art rather than to God who has enabled them. It is as image-bearers of the Creator that artists produce their art. Artistic activities, whether by Christians or non-Christians, bring glory to God, who through the Spirit disperses general gifts to humanity. God sends His rain upon the evil and the good; His sun rises on the just and the unjust. Shakespeare received his abilities from God, yet he worked intensely to conceive his plays.

The Lord has given us freely all good things to enjoy, including the arts that glorify Him. However, people often pervert their gifts and even blaspheme God through them. Here, of course, discernment and awareness are needed in evaluating works of art. Heaven's view is very different from this world's.

When we have mentioned writing this book to others, the response has often been: "Have you included George Sand or Virginia Woolf?" "What about Eudora Welty?" Now and then someone suggests a writer unfamiliar to us. With a smile, our answer is: "We are writing about our favorites, whom we have read over and over again. Perhaps you should write your own book and include all the ones we have omitted."

We are deeply loyal to our outstanding Crossway publishers and are grateful for their invaluable help in our writing lives. We have been extremely fortunate, as it can be very difficult to find a publisher.

There is a long list of remarkable creative people who have found it necessary to publish their own works. Jane Austen paid to have her novel *Sense and Sensibility* printed. The Brontës put up the money for their poetry book. Elizabeth Barrett Browning's father paid to have her early poetry published. Vinnie Dickinson paid to have Emily's poetry brought out after Emily's death.

Beatrice Potter financed her first book, *Peter Rabbit*, as well as *The Tailor of Gloucester*. Christina Rossetti's grandfather paid to have her early poems printed, a great incentive to Christina's creativity.

Gertrude Stein paid to have *Three Lives* printed and, with her friend Alice Toklas, even started a publishing company to publish other works by Gertrude. Edgar Allan Poe published his first poems at his own expense. William Thackeray did the same with *Vanity Fair*, as well as Walt Whitman with *Leaves of Grass*.

The list goes on. We even had one book, *Absolutely and the Golden Eggs*, printed in Switzerland, which was later brought out by Good News Publishers, now Crossway Books. Seeing one's name in print is a great encouragement to persevere. If *you* are unable to find a publisher, *do it yourself*. It could be a good investment.

LOUISA MAY ALCOTT

1832-1888

My Prayer

To smooth the rough and thorny way
Where other feet begin to tread;
To feed some hungry soul each day
With sympathy's sustaining bread.

Louisa May Alcott

When Louisa Alcott hesitantly submitted *Little Women* for publication, the publisher's first thought after he read the manuscript was to tell the author as gently as possible that her work was unacceptable. But he had some qualms about his judgment and decided to show the manuscript to his nieces.

Immediately they loved the book, and their enthusiasm convinced him he was wrong. Readers have continued to enjoy *Little Women* since its publication in 1868 because the characters are flesh-and-blood people, sometimes irritable and difficult, but never failing in their warm affection for each other. This enduring family story is as genuine a taste of realism, truth, and simplicity as American literature has produced.

However, there was a long, hard apprenticeship of writing, as well as struggling against poverty and illness before Louisa May realized her ambition to write a book of lasting value. *Little Women* is basically the story of her own family—their trials, sorrows, disappointments, and joys.

In order to enjoy this novel even more fully, one needs to learn about the Alcott family. Louisa's father, Bronson Alcott (1799-1888), was a noted philosopher and educational reformer. Along with his close friend Ralph

Waldo Emerson (1803-1882), he was a leader in the movement called transcendentalism, as well as an outspoken abolitionist. He was a visionary and above all a teacher, yet impractical. He never knew where his socks or money were, but he always could locate his books. Bronson Alcott was a dreamer and invested in many idealistic projects that failed. In one of his extended western lecture tours, he returned home having earned one dollar. Like a balloon Bronson floated in space while his family held him with strings of reality on earth.

When Abba May decided to marry handsome, blue-eyed Bronson, friends hinted that the young man was "not very practical," and that he would never "make his way." Although it was a happy marriage, Abba May was perplexed by the scarcity of money, and she sought to escape poverty through practical hard work. Like her mother, Louisa May later felt deeply the family trials and years of poverty caused by Bronson.

Louisa May and her older sister Anna were born in Germantown, Pennsylvania, where Bronson taught in a Quaker community. There is something in earlier Quaker family life that is not matched anywhere else. In those days Quakers were cut off from music, dancing, theaters, and gaiety of the social sort. Simple amusements were all within the family, and there was great comradeship between parents and children. The Alcott family always carried with them this early Quaker influence.

In 1834 the Alcotts moved to Boston where Bronson Alcott opened the Temple School. Another daughter, Elizabeth, was born here. Louisa, an independent, lively child full of energy, loved to roam about Boston Common. One day she accidentally fell into the frog pond and almost drowned. A young black boy plunged into the water, dragged her to shore, and then slipped away. She never knew his name but always remembered his kindness. Louisa was strongly antislavery with a burning sense of the injustice done to blacks. She said slavery was America's most terrible mistake.

At first the Temple School was a success. Five years later a little black girl entered as a pupil because Bronson insisted that his school be open to all children. Indignant parents withdrew their children, and

Bronson was forced to close the school. He never had the heart to found another one.

In 1840, encouraged by Emerson, who also helped the Alcotts financially, the family moved to Concord. It should be noted that in the first twenty-eight years of Louisa's life, the Alcotts moved twenty-nine times, often because of monetary difficulties. The fourth daughter, Abba May, was born in the bare little Hasmer Cottage at Concord.

Their father taught the girls in their early years while their mother worked very, very hard to sustain the family. Bronson loved *Pilgrim's Progress* and made it a fundamental part of his children's education. He also read the Bible out loud to them and taught them a great deal about nature. Reading aloud at night was part of the children's delightful instruction.

Louisa first attended public school in Concord when she was fourteen. Before this, while her father discussed philosophy with Emerson and Henry Thoreau, Emerson gave Louisa the freedom to read in his library. Hungering for knowledge, she would curl up in one of his comfortable chairs and read many of the great classics. She idolized Emerson, who in his simple manner wrote on a board because he never owned a desk. He said of Louisa May, "She is, and is to be, the poet of children. She knows their angels."

In early life Emerson had faced poverty and sickness. His father, a Unitarian minister, died young leaving his wife to raise five sons. Like his father, Emerson became a Unitarian minister, but a year later took up a career in literature and philosophy. He was the leader among New England Unitarians who formed the mystical religion of transcendentalism.

Emerson attacked historic Christianity and favored a religion founded on nature, optimism, and individualism. He maintained that the fall of Adam was a false teaching. The transcendentalists believed that human beings should find truth within themselves, that individuals should reject the authority of Christianity and gain knowledge of God through reason. This false doctrine had tragic consequences, including influencing poet Emily Dickinson to turn away from Christianity.

Without the triune God of the Bible, truth is lost—the truth of the universe.

Louisa also had nature lessons from her neighbor Henry Thoreau. Bronson had helped him build his hut at Walden Pond. Thoreau spoke of "washing days" of rain and fog and of a cobweb as a handkerchief dropped by a fairy. He told Louisa that wherever men lived, there was a story to be told. These observations stirred the girl's imagination.

Nineteen miles from Boston, the village of Concord, with its neat, white houses, had been founded by Puritans in 1635. It was a revolutionary center where minutemen rallied to oppose British rule. On April 19, 1775, there was a brief battle at Concord's North Bridge, which Emerson called "the shot heard 'round the world."

In the 1800s the Alcotts' friends and neighbors included Ralph Waldo Emerson, Margaret Fuller, Nathaniel Hawthorne, and Henry Thoreau. All these people influenced Louisa May Alcott and helped to form her ideas about politics and social reform.

Before and during the Civil War, Concord became a station in the Underground Railroad established to help free slaves. The most famous supporter of this famous escape route, Harriet Tubman, was able to free hundreds of slaves, including her own parents. The Alcotts, who had always fed the poor at their home, also assisted runaway slaves. Once the whole family caught smallpox from a beggar Mrs. Alcott fed.

At an early age Louisa began to help support the family by working as a seamstress, a household servant, and a teacher. She even started a school in a barn to teach Emerson's children. Impatient and rebellious, hating household work and longing for independence, she assumed the task of keeping her treasured family secure and happy.

In her day it was considered almost a disgrace for a young woman other than a pauper to work for a living. Only teaching was permissible. Louisa gallantly and with great determination went her own way and eventually triumphed over all these restrictions. She refused to be defeated.

As a girl Louisa kept a diary and wrote poetry. Even in childhood she invented and wrote stories in every spare moment. Like Dickens, one of her favorite authors, she loved putting on theatricals. She was author-director and also acted in them with hilarious enthusiasm. At one time she thought of going on the stage to earn a living, but nothing came of it. Encouraged by her mother, Louisa wrote a drama and then stories in her little upstairs room, as her mind teemed with ideas. With maternal pride, her mother said, "You are going to be like Shakespeare."

Her first published book, *Flower Fables* (1885), consisted of fairy tales she had made up to tell Emerson's daughter. From that time on Louisa's pen was rarely idle. When one starts writing books and sees one's name in print, it is hard to stop.

After countless moves the Alcotts bought Orchard House in Concord, hoping that it would be a permanent home. While it was being repaired, they lived at Hillside, the home of the Hawthornes and later the setting for *Little Women*. Here the beloved sister Elizabeth, who had suffered poor health for years because of typhoid fever, was tenderly nursed by Mrs. Alcott and Louisa. Elizabeth died in her mother's arms, free at last from suffering.

Because she was vigorous, hopeful, cheerful, and sympathetic, Louisa had been called a good nurse by Elizabeth. In 1862 Louisa went as a Union nurse to the Georgetown section of Washington, D.C., in spite of pestilence and infectious diseases that ravaged the army camp. Conditions there were shocking to the young girl. The dirty hospital had once been an old run-down hotel. Her tiny room was bitterly cold, dreary, and bare, with broken window panes—in sharp contrast to her neat home in Concord.

Horribly wounded soldiers arrived continually amid the terrible smells of unwashed bodies, infected wounds, and gangrene. Soon she was assigned as superintendent and night nurse of a large ward, her hours being from midnight until midday. She made her rounds every hour in case someone had died. A rare nurse without surgical skills, she had to wash dirty soldiers who were suffering from awful wounds and diseases such as typhoid, and her duties called her in every direction. She realized there was much to write about, so she sent detailed letters to her family.

Louisa fell desperately ill of typhoid fever after a month or so of nursing. In her delirium she hardly recognized her father, who took her home to the loving care of her family. She was very ill for several months. Her strength had been broken, and she was never completely well after that. Yet her nearness to death taught her the value of life.

As she slowly recovered, she was urged to add stories to the letters she had written to her family as a nurse in Washington. These were published with the title *Hospital Sketches* in 1863. Although carelessly written, they were timely and warmly received by the public.

At the time, Louisa was worn out, thought herself a failure, and began to feel she never wanted to write again. The success of *Hospital Sketches* was the encouragement she needed. She now determined to support herself and her family by writing.

Publishers began to request her writings. She was often in Boston where she decided to seek her fortune single-handed. Determined to sell her work, she wrote trivial potboilers to earn a pittance. However, she was gaining skill, as her pen was nearly always busy writing books and letters. She had to write, even when weak and unwell, to distract her mind.

An editor told Louisa she should stick to her teaching—she would never be a writer. Louisa responded, "I *will* be a writer!" Her persistence paid off in the publication of her book *Moods* in 1864. She was ambitious, an overcomer. Yet with these soaring hopes, she was often disappointed in life.

She once said disappointment must be good for her since she got so much of it. Unbearably lonely in Boston and disheartened, she heard a sermon by Theodore Parker titled "Laborious Young Women." That message was a turning point in her life. She believed she understood ever after who God is and felt His vital presence.

In 1865 she accompanied an invalid to Europe as a nurse-companion and remained there a year. She enjoyed traveling in England, Germany, France, and Switzerland in spite of the cranky invalid, although she was homesick for her family. In Vevey, Switzerland, she met an eighteen-year-old Polish refugee, and they became fast friends. She later wrote of him as Laurie in *Little Women*.

On her return to New England, Thomas Niles of Roberts Brothers

Publishers suggested she write a book for girls. She replied, "I don't know anything about girls except just ourselves." "Well then," responded Niles, "write about your own family." At first she refused, but spurred on by poverty, she settled at Orchard House in May 1868 and started to work on her most important venture, *Little Women.*

Never commonplace, *Little Women* is the simple, wholesome account of Louisa's own family, as the Marches are really the Alcotts. It depicts a warm, loving family with four daughters in the setting of Hillside. The power of the book is in its lead character Jo, who in real life was Louisa.

Louisa's opinion of herself was humble. Always mistrusting her abilities, she tells frankly of every negative feature in Jo's appearance—her awkwardness, thorny moods, flashes of temper, headstrong mistakes, and her longing to be a boy. Yet Jo is lovable and more real than any of the other characters. Louisa herself was a magnificent person, not imitating others but insisting on being herself. At last, with the help of Thomas Niles, she found her style, her fame, and her fortune at the age of thirty-seven.

Soon the whole country was reading *Little Women.* After years of struggle, at last she was a success—famous, greatly loved, and prosperous. She was generous with the prosperity that had come to her, especially to her own family. Her mother, after years of hard work, had grown feeble, so Louisa fixed a big sunny room for her and put in central heating at Orchard House. She did everything possible to make her family comfortable but did little for herself.

Louisa had no inclination toward matrimony, as her heart was bound up in her work and her family. She said that she had decided to settle down as a permanent old maid. In youth she had no money, and now that she had money, she had little time or health to enjoy the freedom. Fame drew many people to her. When reporters arrived at the door, Louisa, dressed as a servant, would say, "Miss Alcott is out of town."

She knew her mind was a treasure house of tales. She sold many short stories to magazines, especially to *Atlantic Monthly,* and continued writing novels such as *Little Men, Jo's Boys, An Old-fashioned Girl, Under the Lilacs,* and so on.

Hard-working as ever, Louisa had a cheery voice and laugh, gave an unfailing impression of courage and good spirits, and possessed instant sympathy with the joys and troubles of other people. She had a strong character with an earnest purpose.

When her mother, to whom she had been so close, died in Louisa's arms, some of the warmth was gone out of her life. In describing her mother as Mrs. March in *Little Women,* she said, "It is all true, only not half good enough."

After her mother's death, Louisa lived in Boston where she enjoyed going to the theater whenever possible. Then well-known, she plunged into the vortex of activities aimed at gaining voting rights for women and promoting the temperance movement.

Her artist sister, May, whom she had supported, married a Swiss and lived in Europe. After the birth of their child, Louisa May Nieriker, nick-named Lulu, May died leaving Louisa to raise the baby. From then on the New England household revolved around Lulu.

All through her life Louisa May Alcott had constantly gone beyond her strength in spite of frail health, and at last she paid for it. On March 6, 1888, incessant overwork finally caused her death at age fifty-six. Her father had died two days before. Louisa May Alcott had triumphed, not only in loyally providing for her beloved family but also in writing books of lasting value.

BIBLIOGRAPHY

Meigs, Cornelia. *Invincible Louisa.* Boston: Little, Brown and Co., 1968.

Stern, Madeleine B. *Louisa May Alcott.* University of Oklahoma Press, 1985.

RECOMMENDED READING

> *Little Women*
> *Little Men*
> *Jo's Boys*
> *Under the Lilacs*

JANE AUSTEN
1775-1817

I must keep to my own style.

Jane Austen

Only one set of books deserves to be read over and over and over—the sixty-six books of the Bible. Some books should be read once and some not at all, but Jane Austen's six novels can be read many times with increasing delight.

Jane was the seventh child of a country clergyman and spent her days almost entirely within the family circle. About this narrow world she wrote lasting literature because she understood her limitations. Her "novels of manners" are among the best-loved works of English fiction. Along with the Brontës and George Eliot, she is considered among the greatest of women novelists.

Not everyone will appreciate the writings of Jane Austen, finding them too limited and confined. She said, "Two or three families in a country village is the very thing to work on." Her novels are mostly set in the country and describe the small world of the gentry with which she was familiar. As author Virginia Woolf said, "She never trespassed beyond her boundaries."

With humorous modesty she wrote to a favorite nephew, Edward, "There is a little bit of ivory on which I work with so fine a brush as produces little effect after much labor." From personal experience she wrote domestic novels about well-fed people in quiet corners. This self-imposed limitation for her was great gain. "I must keep to my own style," she maintained. As Somerset Maugham said in *Ten Novels and Their Authors*, his choice of the ten greatest novels: "Nothing very much happens in her books, but when you come to the bottom of the page, you eagerly turn to learn what will happen next." Austen is wonderfully readable, and her dialogue is masterful. "Her books are pure entertainment," said Maugham.

Jane Austen was born in 1775. One of eight children, she began and ended her life in Hampshire. Her father, George Austen, was rector of the Steventon church. She belongs to a large company of famous children of clergymen—Joseph Addison, Samuel Coleridge, Thomas Macaulay, the Brontës, Alfred Tennyson, William Cowper, Friedrich Nietzsche, the Wesleys, Isaac Watts, Lewis Carroll, Carolus Linnaeus, Vincent Van Gogh, Matthew Arnold, and Frances Ridley Havergal.

Perhaps one reason for the creativity of these people was the advantage of reading in their fathers' libraries. A writer must love to read, and it can be one step from reading to writing. We often think of Francis Schaeffer, the clergyman who founded L'Abri Fellowship, and his wife, Edith, and their amazing creativity that has flowed on to their children and to those of us influenced by them throughout the world.

Both parents of Jane Austen were exceptional—happily married, energetic, kindly, yet disciplined. They mainly home-schooled their children. George and Cassandra were genuinely fond of their children and took great interest in them. In return the children were devoted to their parents. The family was close-knit, with a high-spirited, cheerful home life that included no luxuries.

The children were taught good sense, good manners, reasonable piety, and a high-spirited sense of fun. They were not in the habit of arguing with each other, but rather delighted in being together. Their social pleasures were dining, dancing, and playing whist (the ancestor of bridge) with friends. By far the most important family to the Austens was their own, including aunts, uncles, cousins, nieces, and nephews. Their sense of family loyalty was profound. "All were in high spirits and disposed to be pleased with each other."

Jane's father was mainly responsible for her education, and from him she acquired a love of literature. He taught her to read among the 500 volumes of his library. She admired Samuel Johnson—called him "my dear Samuel Johnson." She appreciated his good sense, humor, and Anglican piety. She also admired Goldsmith, Addison, Richardson, Fielding (she read novels avidly, such as those by Fanny Burney), and Cowper (who wrote nature poetry). Encouraged by her father, she turned from reading to writing. Before she was in her teens, she was spending much time writing. Already in these juvenile works we hear her distinct voice of ironic humor seeking to amuse her family and friends.

From her mother she inherited a quick wit and realistic judgment. Cassandra was intelligent, hard-working, cheerful, contented, and possessed a bright sense of comedy. She was a strict disciplinarian in the household and relieved boredom by telling amusing stories about the pigs and chickens. Jane always fell in with her mother's wishes. The parents trusted God for their children. The mother educated the young ones, and the father took over when they were older. Jane received more education than most women of her time, although her spelling is amusingly different—"Swisserland, chuse, freindship."

A great feature of Austen family life was the father reading out loud to his children—a measure of the high standard of culture in the home. Jane, who truly was a comic genius, also read her writings out loud to entertain her fun-loving family. They were highly amused, and there were continual outbursts of laughter. Her impulse in writing was to make her readers laugh, and she hardly wrote a paragraph without the glint of a smile. She poked fun at the superficialities of polite society, probably including word pictures of neighbors and acquaintances. She realized how rarely comedy is accorded the respect it deserves as literature.

Her niece Marianne recalled how Aunt Jane would sit quietly sewing (she loved needlework) and then suddenly would burst out laughing, jump up, and run across the room to a table where paper and pens were lying. Jane would quickly write down something and then go back to the fireplace and go on working as before.

Except for brief visits away from home, Jane spent her first twenty-five years in her father's rectory at Steventon. She is one of the few persons of genius to reach the age of eighteen without feeling lonely, rebellious, or misunderstood. She was a sprightly, fun-loving young woman possessing wit, beauty, and determination. Her genius was favored by the quiet, friendly village life she knew.

English countryside was at its loveliest in the time of the Austens. In such a secure, stable framework she had time and tranquillity to follow her literary gift without being troubled with world events about her. She disliked dwelling on "odious subjects."

Most of the days of Jane Austen were passed within her circle of family and friends. A special friend was Martha Lloyd, who was sweet-tempered with a mind deeply impressed concerning the truth of Christianity. Jane had two highly successful brothers who were admirals in the navy, Frank and Charles. They often brought home outside news, especially during the brutal years of the Napoleonic Wars. Her brother Frank, who later became head of the entire English navy, was a favorite of Lord Nelson.

Jane never married, but she did have an opportunity to do so. One evening while visiting in the magnificent Bigg-Wither mansion, the wealthy, silly son, Harris, abruptly asked Jane to marry him. Startled, she said yes. After a sleepless night and with an admirable sense of integrity, she changed her answer to no. The possibility of a luxurious yet loveless marriage was unthinkable to Jane. She left the mansion soon after, upsetting many of the other guests.

The circumstances of life may also have prevented her from marrying. It is thought that Jane fell in love with a clergyman who suddenly died at an early age.

The creative impulse often fulfilled in the roles of wife and mother, in Jane Austen was fulfilled through her art. She did not need her own children to make her happy. "My books are my children," she declared. Instead of attaching herself to a husband, she left us her inimitable novels. Sometimes marriage can end one's creativity, as in the lives of Charlotte Brontë and Beatrix Potter.

The person closest to Jane was her older sister, Cassandra, whom

Jane loved and respected. "If Cassandra were going to have her head cut off," Mrs. Austen once claimed, "Jane would insist on sharing her fate." The two sisters shared the same bedroom. With unfailing devotion Cassandra listened carefully, often with bursts of laughter, as Jane read her manuscripts out loud. Cassandra was always a necessary help in Jane's writing. As a critic and censor, she was not too easy to please, yet she offered many encouraging words. Besides her sister, Jane's brothers, nieces (Fanny and Anna particularly), and nephews remained the central people in her personal life.

Some of the best information we have about Jane is her letters, because she kept close contact with her family, especially Cassandra, by mail. Letters are a great source of knowledge, so we should be careful not to throw them all away.

Jane hardly ever wrote a letter that did not bring a laugh or a smile. She often commented about the weather and was not fond of depressing rainy days. On one occasion she wrote to Cassandra, "July begins unpleasantly with us, cold and showery, but it is often a baddish month." In another letter she observed, "What dreadful hot weather we have! It keeps me in a continual state of inelegance."

Jane was not inclined to talk about herself. The subject did not seem to interest her. Furthermore, she always kept quiet about her literary activities, and her novels were published anonymously. She had an obsession about keeping her identity as an author private, although she was a born artist. She was too modest to believe her novels would be read long after her death, for she never had much confidence in the merit of her books. Unsentimental, she kept her writing realistic and humorous.

Jane Austen spent her first twenty-five years in Steventon and five unwilling years in Bath. But it was Bath that had much influence on her writing, as five of her six novels have scenes there. Then there were three unsettled, not very happy years in Southampton. Finally at age thirty-four she settled in Chawton to spend the rest of her life as a dedicated author, although it was a secret dedication.

In Chawton she had everything she valued right there—family, garden, the Hampshire countryside, and the products of her imagination.

She began to revise her early novels almost as soon as she moved there, and she determined to risk publication at her own expense. According to biographer Park Honan, "The Chawton years were the settled, fulfilling, productive years, but all that went before was not wasted. . . . Secure in her home, she finally found the right conditions in which to exercise her genius. In these Chawton rooms she produced the most delightful comedy in our language since Shakespeare."

Chawton cottage is now an excellent museum. In the nearby village of Selborne the famous naturalist Gilbert White lived and wrote his great book, *The Natural History of Selborne*. Just down the road from Selborne is Greatham, the English branch of L'Abri Fellowship.

At Chawton Jane helped with the housework and gardening, did needlework (usually for the poor), and rose early to practice the piano before preparing breakfast. She played loud marches, which probably roused Mrs. Austen's ducks and chickens.

She had an acute need for daily music. She was probably not aware of her contemporaries, Haydn and Mozart, though their glorious quartets with their neoclassic elegance, proportion, and humor remind us of her writing style.

After breakfast she spent the morning reading and writing at a small mahogany desk while looking out on the busy Chawton street. Cassandra and Mrs. Austen did most of the housework so Jane could have freedom to write. Jane's primary interest in social life was as a sharp-eyed observer, and all she saw stirred her imagination. She wrote in the combined front hall and dining room on small pieces of paper that she could quickly slip into a desk drawer if the kitchen door creaked in warning of someone's coming. There was a constant flow of visiting relatives and friends. Here for the next nine years, she revised, rewrote, and polished her six novels—the great works of her mature years.

After writing her first three novels, she was probably discouraged at not finding a publisher, for recognition came to her slowly. Finally, with the help of her favorite brother, Henry, who dealt with her publishers and was ever a great help, *Sense and Sensibility* was published in 1811 at her own expense. It was signed, "By a lady."

There is something magical in seeing one's writing in print, and it is an encouragement to persevere. Two amusing quotes from *Sense and Sensibility*: "After some time spent in saying little and doing less, Lady Middleton sat down to casino." At a dinner party: "No poverty of any kind except of conversation appeared—but there the deficiency was considerable. John Dashwood had not much to say for himself that was worth saying, and his wife had still less."

In 1813 *Pride and Prejudice* was published and met with instant success. It was considered her greatest achievement with its mastery of dialogue and comedy her highest and finest. She spoke of this novel to Cassandra as "her darling child." Her family, to whom she read it out loud, were enchanted.

However, because of her obsession that no one should recognize her as the author, the book was published anonymously. The famous opening sentence sets the stage for the entire book: "It is a truth universally acknowledged that a single man in possession of a good fortune must be in want of a wife." The heroine, Elizabeth, with her lively mind is one of Jane's most vivacious, spirited creations and the one Jane liked best. Her portraits of women have rarely been surpassed.

Another of her memorable characters is the obnoxious Mr. Collins. Jane knew a variety of pompous clergymen, so she did not have to invent a character. She put down what she saw in real life.

Some readers have been troubled over Jane's concern about money in her novels, but she was a realist and knew the importance of it. As Proverbs 10:15 says, money is a defense. She wrote in a letter to Cassandra, "Single women have a dreadful propensity to be poor, which is one very strong argument in favor of matrimony." She and Cassandra learned to make the best of hardships because they realized they were "poor relations" dependent on others in the family.

Jane and Cassandra visited wealthy relatives at some of the great mansions in southern England, so Jane was acquainted with the comfortable, well-ordered lives of these people. She was amused by England's obsession with gardening. Transportation was poor; therefore, visits to country houses were generally long. Concerning her brother

Edward's magnificent home, Godmersham, she wrote, "Kent is the only place for happiness. Everybody is rich there." Jane was financially dependent on her family all her life.

Each of Jane's novels is different. *Mansfield Park*, published in 1814, is considered one of the most profound novels of the nineteenth century. Her evangelical heroine, Fanny Price, with her regard for moral virtue, is a potent force for good at Mansfield Park. Fanny is a person of deep moral conviction and a true Christian.

Jane too was a person of moral intensity. From her father she learned that true religion is the basis of civil society. As a Christian she learned to be useful and do her duty, insisting on self-discipline and right conduct. Several commentators have pointed out the influence of her faith on her work:

> A stoical Christian faith underlies all her novels and gives them that moral confidence, a severity and certainty which allow her comic talent to flourish lightly.
>
> C. S. Lewis

> Faith is not discussed in Jane Austen's novels, because the author felt it too important: it was not to be mixed with jokes, but implicit. Hence her comic work rests on religion, without arguing for it.
>
> Park Honan

> Miss Austen has the merit of being evidently a Christian writer, a merit enhanced . . . by her religion being not at all obtrusive.
>
> Richard Whately

Jane's brother Henry described her as thoroughly religious and devout. She read sermons for pleasure as well as for edification. She practiced her faith and regularly attended the Anglican church. She did not care for "noisy religion"; her concern was for truth.

The following is one of her prayers:

> Father of Heaven, whose goodness has brought us in safety to the close of this day, dispose our hearts in fervent prayer. Another day is now gone and added to those for which we were before accountable. Teach us, Almighty Father, to consider this solemn truth, as we should do,

that we may feel the importance of every day and every hour as it passes, and earnestly strive to make a better use of what Thy goodness may yet bestow on us, than we have done of the time past. Incline us, O God, to consider our fellow creatures with kindness.

After *Mansfield Park* Jane wrote *Emma*, a matchless treasure of English wit. It is the most pastoral and happiest of her novels in describing the beauty of the changing seasons and Jane's intense love for England. At one point the charming yet snobbish Emma says, "A young farmer, whether on horseback or on foot, is the very last sort of person to raise my curiosity. The yeomanry is precisely the order of people with whom I feel I can have nothing to do."

Biographer Park Honan mused, "It may be said (from our modern viewpoint) that most of the English people from beggars and thieves up to the nobility were snobs." Yet Jane is the great "anti-snob" of people of letters. Unsentimental, never more than a little below her best, she wonderfully described her society of the eighteenth century with ironic humor.

As her fame grew, she often visited her brother Henry in London where she learned about contemporary high society. She cared little for London or the distresses of such a meaningless social life. In *Pride and Prejudice* she wrote of London as a hiding place for the guilty and a constant threat to country life. "We do not look in great cities for the best morality" (*Mansfield Park*). She loved her countryside, convinced that its beauty was close to the joys of heaven.

At the end of her life the self-effacing Jane Austen was accepted among the finest of living authors although she had earned less than 800 pounds for all her work. *Persuasion* and *Northanger Abbey* were published after her death, thanks to Henry, though the latter was a high-spirited, sparkling early work. To quote from *Northanger Abbey*: "Where did you get that quiz of a hat; it makes you look like an old witch."

And another quote: "Mrs. Allen was one of that numerous class of females whose society can raise no other emotion than surprise at there being any men in the world who would like them well enough to marry them." Jane's was a unique, uncluttered, crisp style without clichés. All her novels end happily.

When she became ill with Addison's disease, she moved with her sister Cassandra to Winchester to be closer to doctors. In March 1817 she laid down her pen never to write again. Gradually losing strength, she died at age forty-one with her head on Cassandra's shoulder. She had calmly accepted the fact that death was coming.

Jane's death came at the height of her powers. Cassandra, who faithfully attended Jane until her death, wrote to a relative: "I have lost a treasure, such a sister, such a friend as never can have been surpassed. She was the sun of my life, the gilder of every pleasure, the soother of every sorrow. I had not a thought concealed from her, and it is as if I had lost part of myself."

At Jane's request she was buried in Winchester Cathedral. Henry said, "In the whole catalogue of its mighty dead, the cathedral does not contain the ashes of a brighter genius or a sincerer Christian."

Jane Austen was the delight of her family, and today her books belong to the world of classics. As biographer Ian Watt said, "Austen's literary skill and moral understanding convert her novels into something much greater than they at first seem."

BIBLIOGRAPHY

Austen, Jane. *Jane Austen: Selected Letters.* Oxford: Oxford University Press, 1985.

Cecil, David. *A Portrait of Jane Austen.* New York: Penguin Books, 1978.

Honan, Park. *Jane Austen: Her Life.* New York: St. Martin's Griffin, 1987.

Lane, Maggie. *Jane Austen's England.* London: Robert Hale Ltd., 1996.

RECOMMENDED READING

Northanger Abbey
Sense and Sensibility
Pride and Prejudice
Mansfield Park
Emma
Persuasion

THE BRONTËS

1816-1855 / 1818-1848 / 1820-1849

*Patrick Brontë's influence upon his children was profound.
Directly and indirectly his style of life and deeply held
views were to shape their development as people and as writers.
To know them we must first try to know him.*

Brian Wilks

After the death of Patrick Brontë's last child, Charlotte, friends urged him to put a stop to the many versions and legends of her life being circulated in England. He agreed that Charlotte's friend Elizabeth Gaskell was the one best qualified to write her story. In 1857 Mrs. Gaskell's *Life of Charlotte Brontë* was published, and it is one of the greatest biographies of the nineteenth century. That was the beginning of a veritable stream of books about this unusual and brilliant family.

In much of what has been written about the Brontës, Patrick comes across in a bad light. He is often portrayed as a hypochondriac recluse, a selfish, austere, eccentric tyrant, or a narrow-minded Victorian preacher. Brian Wilks, in his excellent and carefully researched book, *The Brontës*, shows us that the Reverend Patrick Brontë has been a much misunderstood and maligned man.

One of the typical stories passed on to illustrate Patrick's "eccentricity" involves the pistol he shot off every morning from his bedroom window. The true explanation is simple. It was not unusual for a householder in the 1800s to keep firearms nearby. He loaded the gun at night and kept it by his bedside in case of danger and then discharged it in the morning when it was no longer needed. Another "eccentricity" was that he allowed no curtains in Haworth parsonage for fear of fire.

Patrick, the first of ten children, was born in Ireland in 1777 on St. Patrick's Day. His parents were peasants who eked out a poor living and were unable to read or write. His father, a farmer, was thought to be a "storyteller." How Patrick learned to read and write no one knows, but by the time he was sixteen, he was teaching in a public school. Eventually he became a tutor in the home of a Presbyterian minister, the Reverend Thomas Tighe. Being in the home of an educated person with a fine library had a great influence on his life. A sidelight: When John Wesley was on his regular preaching tours in Ireland, he always stayed with the Tighes.

At the age of twenty-five Patrick entered St. John's College, Cambridge, with the help of Rev. Tighe. Living frugally and working hard, he was also the servant of a nobleman. He was helped financially by Wesleyan Methodists, as well as by the great missionary Henry Martyn and by William Wilberforce, who was instrumental in the abolition of slavery in the British Empire. The red-headed, ambitious Irishman exercised considerable self-discipline and did well in college. In 1807 he was ordained a minister of the Church of England in the Royal Chapel at St. James Palace.

Patrick moved rapidly from one curacy to another. He also began to write poetry, and in 1811 his first book, *Cottage Poems*, was published. The purpose of the book was to provide a simple "reader" for semiliterate poor people. He had a burden for the lower classes of society, and all his life he was involved in helping to educate them.

In 1812 Patrick married Maria Branwell, a devout Christian and a lovely lady. In almost every respect her childhood and upbringing was in contrast to Patrick's long, hard struggle. Even though they had only a short life together—Marie died of cancer nine years after the marriage—it was a good and happy union. There were six children—Maria, Elizabeth, Charlotte, Patrick Branwell, Emily Jane, and Anne.

In 1820 the family moved to Haworth in Yorkshire. Haworth had been the center of the great Wesleyan revival where Grimshaw and the Wesleys preached to overflowing congregations. Having heard glowing accounts of the revival, Patrick was thrilled to be called to this well-known church. (Other notable Christians whose names are associated with Haworth are John Newton, George Whitefield, and the Countess of Huntingdon.) Haworth was to be the home and church of the Brontë family for the rest of their lives.

The living room window of the parsonage looked out on the church and graveyard. It was a very unhealthy, cold, uncomfortable place to live, but the menace of the cemetery meant nothing to the children. It was their world, and the unique setting dominated and shaped their imaginations. Close by their home lay the small town of Haworth, and beyond stretched the rugged moors and hills of Yorkshire.

All the children loved wandering outdoors. In the changes of weather and seasons, the moors were their exhilarating playground. In one of her poems Emily spoke for the family:

> *There is a spot mid barren hills*
> *Where winter howls and drives the rain . . .*
> *The house is old, the trees are bare . . .*
> *The mute bird sitting on the stone,*
> *The dark moss dripping from the wall,*
> *The thorn trees gaunt, the walks o'ergrown—*
> *I love them, how I love them all.*

Charlotte wrote about Emily: "She found in the bleak solitude many and dear delights, and the best loved was liberty." Her spirit soared on the lonely moors of Yorkshire.

Before moving to Haworth, Patrick published two more books. One of them, *The Cottage of the Woods*, was printed in three editions. The Brontë children grew up with a father actively engaged in writing. Patrick wrote the first Brontë novel to appear in print (now *long* forgotten), so as Charlotte said, "The idea of being authors was as natural to them [the children] as walking, and one they never forsook."

At a remarkably early age the Brontë children were omnivorous readers and were recording prose and poetry in tiny homemade booklets. Charlotte and Branwell were writing about the imaginary exotic world of Angria, while Emily and Anne were involved in the more austere saga of Gondal. Their youthful output of literature was enormous. Although of no intrinsic value, it was evidence of the astonishing precocity of the young family. They lived in a world of make-believe adventure.

After living in Haworth scarcely twelve months, Maria, the beloved wife and mother, died. She had been through a long period of intense suffering. Her last words were, "Oh, God, my poor children; Oh, God, my poor children."

Patrick was stunned. He wrote in detail of his sorrow but closed the letter with these words: "Maria fell asleep in Jesus, and her soul took its flight to the mansions of glory. During many years she had walked with God."

Maria's older sister Elizabeth, who had come to help nurse Maria, made the difficult decision to stay on after her sister's death to help run the parsonage and bring up the children. A devoted Christian, Elizabeth had a sense of responsibility and duty. Her influence for good on the children was profound.

Elizabeth helped to establish a high moral tone in the home. She obviously needed her privacy and at times kept to her room, but that room also became a classroom as Aunt Branwell helped to educate the Brontë children. They not only read lessons and learned to embroider and to turn collars and cuffs of shirts and dresses (they were obliged to make most of their own clothes), but they were encouraged to discuss current affairs. Patrick too included his children in discussions of recent developments in art and literature and what was happening in the military and in Parliament.

Patrick had his study, and the children's bedroom was also called a study rather than a nursery. The children quickly came to know that privacy should be respected and that it is a treasured commodity of a growing mind.

Patrick was a conscientious minister and active in every sphere of parish life. He had a special interest in the Sunday school program, where not only the Scriptures were taught, but some pupils also learned to read. His children helped by teaching Sunday school.

Charlotte carried food to the poor. Anne wrote a number of hymns that can still be found in some English hymnals. Charlotte wrote the hymn "Winter Stones." When asked one day what the best book in the world was, she answered, "The Bible."

Morning lessons for the children were held in Patrick's study, but by 1824 he decided that the older girls needed a more formal education. Maria, Elizabeth, and later Charlotte and Emily were sent to Cowan Bridge, a newly established school for the daughters of clergymen.

Before a year passed, the girls were suddenly withdrawn from the school because of unsanitary conditions. In May 1825 Maria died of tuberculosis, and soon after that Elizabeth died. All the Brontës were susceptible to this dreadful disease.

The double tragedy following so soon after the death of his wife, as well as the unhealthy environment at Haworth resulting in his frail health, caused Patrick to withdraw further into his study. He sought to remarry several times but was refused. Patrick then prayed that he might remain alive to care for his other four children and spare them the horrors of being poor and unwanted.

Charlotte, Branwell, Emily, and Anne stayed close to each other, for they needed one another to go on in their loneliness and sorrow. The next five years were fruitful as they pored over books and began to find release and excitement in writing. Branwell described their activity as "scribble mania." The game of making little books from scraps of paper or acting out plays was not only entertaining, but was disciplining them for the novels they were to write later.

The Brontës collaborated with each other in creative projects. Many years afterward, Patrick told Mrs. Gaskell:

> As soon as they could read and write, Charlotte and her brother and sisters used to invent little plays of their own, in which the Duke of Wellington, my daughter Charlotte's hero, was sure to come off the conquering hero. When a dispute would not infrequently arise regarding the merits of him, Bonaparte, Hannibal, and Caesar— when the argument rose to its height, I had sometimes to come in and settle the dispute to the best of my judgment.

Even though Charlotte and Emily were at Cowan Bridge only a

short time, it made them all the more appreciative of home. What they cared for most at Haworth were the natural surroundings, especially the moors *and* mental freedom. However, the school left such a deep impression on eight-year-old Charlotte that years later she described every detail of the bitter experience when she wrote about the notorious Lowood School in *Jane Eyre*.

In 1831 Charlotte was sent to Miss Wooler's school at Roe Head. Here she made lasting friendships with Mary Taylor and Ellen Nussey. Her correspondence with Ellen, which continued until her death, has provided much of what we know about Charlotte.

When she came home from Roe Head, she was able to teach her teenage sisters, and for three full years they lived, studied, and wrote at Haworth. Lonely, shy, poor, and sensitive, they occupied themselves with music, drawing, reading, and, above all, writing. They stayed close to home and had few outside friends. Patrick would not let his children associate with the village children. "They kept to themselves." This isolation led to the early development of their imaginations.

In 1836 Charlotte wrote to the famous poet Robert Southey, asking about the possibility of a woman earning a living from writing and enclosing some of her poetry. His response was discouraging: "Literature cannot be the business of a woman's life, and it ought not to be. The more she is engaged in her proper duties, the less leisure she will have for it, even as an accomplishment and a recreation. To these duties you have not yet been called, and when you are, you will be less eager for celebrity." For many years after the receipt of this letter, Charlotte made no attempt to see her name in print.

For financial reasons the sisters decided to start a school, so Charlotte and Emily went to Brussels for further education. Here Charlotte fell in love with a married man, Professor Heger, although she knew it to be wrong and that nothing would ever come of it but her own suffering. Her last novel, *Villette*, is a masterful description of her time in Brussels. Unfortunately when the Brontës opened their school in Haworth, not one pupil came.

Meanwhile Branwell began his career as an artist. He started with enthusiasm, but he was fundamentally weak-willed, unstable, excessive, intemperate, and a habitual romancer. Spoiled by his father, who had educated him to be a genius, he failed at everything he attempted; his life was a series of disgraces. Time after time he returned home from unsuccessful endeavors to make a living. Opium, rum, gin, and worry over his debts took rapid toll on his health. Branwell spent much of his time talking and drinking at the Black Bull Inn. His sisters, who truly loved him, looked on helplessly with anguish and horror.

In 1845 after Aunt Elizabeth Branwell died, and with Patrick ill and Branwell in a deplorable state, the three sisters turned to their writing in a more committed way than ever. It preserved their sanity and helped prevent their falling into despair.

"One day, in the autumn of 1845," Charlotte wrote Ellen, "I accidentally lighted on a . . . volume of verse in my sister Emily's handwriting." Right away Charlotte realized these poems had true literary value (Emily is considered one of the finest women poets in English literature). How should she tell Emily, one of the most private persons who ever lived, that her poetry had been discovered and was worthy to be published?

As Emily raged about her poetry being discovered, Anne quietly produced some of her own poems and wondered if Charlotte would care to read them. "We had very early cherished the dream of one day becoming authors. . . . We agreed to arrange a small selection of our poems, and, if possible, get them printed," continued Charlotte's letter to Ellen. It was Charlotte who took the initiative of doing something about their writing. Choosing the masculine names Currer, Ellis, and Acton Bell, they had the book printed at their own expense, using money inherited from Aunt Branwell. Only two copies sold. "As was to be expected," Charlotte concluded, "neither we nor our poems were at all wanted."

Charlotte had a Protestant reverence for "the uses of adversity" and had great perseverance in spite of life's difficulties. The failure of the poetry book did not crush them. On the contrary, it gave them extra zeal to try something else. They set to work writing *The Professor, Wuthering Heights,* and *Agnes Grey.*

They kept their identities a secret. For years the three had been meeting in the evening in the parlor after family prayers where they enjoyed walking around the table exchanging ideas, discussing the writing they were doing, and reading extracts to each other.

By April 1846 the novels were ready, so they began to mail out their manuscripts for publication. Charlotte, without changing the wrapping paper, struck out the name of one publisher and sent it to another. After the sixth mailing, she found acceptance for Emily's and Anne's manuscripts if they were willing to pay some of the cost of production. When her manuscript was sent to Smith, Elder, and Company, the editor wrote a kind letter refusing the book, but he wondered if Currer Bell had something else to show them.

Meanwhile leaving Emily and Anne to cope with Branwell's drunken bouts, Charlotte accompanied her father to Manchester where he underwent cataract surgery. It was performed without anesthesia, with Charlotte holding her father's hand. Patrick displayed extraordinary patience, but the time of convalescence proved tedious for Charlotte. She was tormented by a toothache, a headache, and anxiety about what was happening at home. In a great effort of will to forget her pain and boredom, she started to write another book—*Jane Eyre*. When published in London in 1847, it was a spectacular success. It was dedicated to William Makepiece Thackeray.

With *Jane Eyre*'s mounting success, Emily and Anne urged Charlotte to tell their father about the publication. According to Mrs. Gaskell, the following conversation took place:

> "Papa, I've been writing a book."
> "Have you, my dear?"
> "Yes, and I want you to read it."
> "I'm afraid it will try my eyes too much."
> "But it is not in manuscript; it is printed."
> "My dear, have you thought of the expense?"

Finally she read him some of the excellent reviews of the book and left him with a copy of *Jane Eyre*.

Later when Patrick came to tea, he said, "Girls, do you know Charlotte has been writing a book, and it is much better than likely?"

When prudish Victorian criticism spread about *Jane Eyre*, Charlotte wrote, "I must have my own way in the matter of writing. . . . I am thankful to God Who gave me this faculty; and it is for me a part of my religion to defend this gift and to profit by its possession."

By 1847 all three sisters had a first work of fiction in print. There was much conjecture as to who Currer, Ellis, and Action Bell really were, so Charlotte and Anne took a train to London to prove to the publisher that they were three sisters. They were unable to persuade Emily to accompany them, as she never liked to leave Haworth.

A clerk told George Smith, the head of the firm that published Charlotte's book, that two ladies, who refused to give their names, wished to see him. As Mr. Smith enjoyed telling the story afterwards: "Two rather quaintly dressed little ladies, pale-faced and anxious-looking, walked into my room. . . . They explained that they had come to help clear up the misunderstanding concerning who wrote *Jane Eyre, Wuthering Heights*, and *Agnes Grey.*"

The following year was tragic. Branwell died of a combination of delirium tremens and tuberculosis, begging his father for forgiveness. Emily caught a cold at Branwell's funeral in September and never left the house again, refusing to see a doctor. After intense suffering, she died in December of tuberculosis at the age of thirty.

Her novel *Wuthering Heights*—that strange and wonderful book—was not well received by the critics. They thought it too wild, especially the phrase, "I am Heathcliff." Today this book is considered one of the finest novels in the English language, and her poetry has been compared with Emily Dickinson's.

Charlotte wrote of Emily: "Simpler than a child, her nature stood alone. I have seen nothing like it; but indeed, I have never seen her parallel in anything." Emily, the most stoic of the sisters, surpassed them in creative intensity and genius. She rarely ventured into the world, had no friends, and hated being away from home with its mental liberty and the freedom of the moors. She did all the ironing and, like Emily Dickinson, made bread. Outward contentment and inward rebellion are expressed in her poem:

> *No coward soul is mine,*
> *No trembler in the world's storm-troubled sphere:*
> *I see Heaven's glories shine*
> *And faith shines equal, arming me from fear.*

After Emily's death, both Anne and their father fell ill. Charlotte wrote to Ellen Nussey: "When we lost Emily, I thought we had drained the very dregs of our cup of trial, but now when I hear Anne cough as Emily coughed, I tremble lest there should be exquisite bitterness to taste."

Anne was modest about her writing: "Such humble talents as God has given me I will endeavor to put to their greatest use." Ill with tuberculosis, she asked to be taken to Scarborough as she loved being near the sea. Accompanied by Charlotte and Ellen Nussey, she died four days after their arrival—at the age of twenty-nine.

Charlotte arranged for Anne to be buried there in order to spare her father another funeral. Patrick, with deep concern for Charlotte, urged her to stay away from Haworth until her health improved. But like Jane Eyre, Charlotte was made of stern stuff and still had strength to fight the battle of life. By June she was back at Haworth, consoling her father and determined to continue her writing.

In the empty parsonage her father still took his meals alone in his room while Charlotte had her solitary meals in the parlor. She wrote in her loneliness, "I do not know how life will pass, but I certainly do feel confidence in Him who has upheld me hitherto."

She was able to calm her grief for Emily, who had loved freedom and independence, by recreating her in *Shirley*, her next novel, which was well received. As in all of Charlotte's novels, the story had a firm moral basis. Even though Charlotte did not preach feminist doctrine, her life and art were an eloquent protest against the cruel and frustrating limitations imposed upon women.

At her father's urging, Charlotte wrote her fourth and last novel,

Villette, considered by some her finest work. While writing the book, she had several proposals of marriage. Since the age of fifteen, she had been acutely conscious of her physical unattractiveness and frail health. Arthur Bell Nicholls, Patrick's curate from Ireland, had loved Charlotte for a long time but was concerned about what her father would say.

When Charlotte told Patrick of Mr. Nicholls's proposal, her father vehemently insisted on a distinct refusal. Later he forced Nicholls to leave Haworth. Yet eighteen months later Charlotte was married to Arthur Bell Nicholls with the understanding that she and her husband would live in the parsonage she both loved and loathed.

Charlotte married Nicholls out of her loneliness, but it proved to be a happy and fulfilling union. One of Patrick's objections was that he felt she was not strong enough for marriage and that pregnancy might prove fatal. In less than a year Charlotte did die at the age of thirty-eight due to complications of pregnancy.

Nicholls stayed on with Patrick, who died at the age of eighty-five. For forty years Patrick had devoted himself to the moral and physical welfare of his parish, while his extraordinary family flourished and then faded about him. He told Mrs. Gaskell that if he had been more calm and conventional, "I should in all probability never have had such children as mine have been."

It is interesting that one of Martha Graham's greatest choreographic works, *Death and Entrances*, portrays the kinship of Charlotte, Emily, Anne, Branwell, and Heathcliff to the wild spirits of the moors.

The novels of the three Brontë sisters are among the most widely read in the English language.

BIBLIOGRAPHY

Poems quoted from Emily Brontë. *Complete Poems of Emily Brontë*. London: Hodder and Stoughton, 1900.

Bently, Phyllis. *The Brontës*. London: Thames and Hudson, 1986.

Gaskell, Elizabeth. *The Life of Charlotte Brontë*. London: J. M. Dent and Sons, 1971.

Lane, Margaret. *The Brontë Story*. London: William Heinemann, Ltd., 1970.

Peters, Margot. *Unquiet Soul*. New York: Doubleday and Co., 1975.

Wilks, Brian. *The Brontës*. New York: Viking Press, 1975.

RECOMMENDED READING

Charlotte Brontë
> *The Professor*
> *Jane Eyre*
> *Shirley*
> *Villette*

Emily Brontë
> *Wuthering Heights*
> *The Complete Poems of Emily Brontë*

Anne Brontë
> *Agnes Grey*
> *The Tenant of Wildfell Hall*

ELIZABETH BARRETT BROWNING
1806-1861

How do I love thee?
Let me count the ways.

Elizabeth Barrett

Elizabeth Barrett's escape from her father's despotic rule, her severe invalidism, and the London climate that was killing her, to a renewal of health and happiness with Robert Browning in the sunshine of Florence, Italy, is one of the noblest love stories of all time. These lovers were two of the most famous poets of their day. That they were able to record the progress of their feelings in some of the most eloquent love letters and poems in the English language has made their romance immortal. The cruel opposition of Elizabeth's father, Edward Moulton-Barrett, has insured high drama in this story.

A friend of Robert Browning's described Elizabeth's father as "one of those tyrannical, arbitrary, puritanical rascals who go sleekly about the world, canting Calvinism abroad and acting despotism at home." Edward Barrett attended Harrow and later Cambridge for a short time but left because he could not tolerate the high spirits of his contemporaries. Already he was being described as "difficult, insensitive, self-willed and isolated."

At nineteen Edward fell in love with the beautiful, clever Mary Clarke, five years his senior, and soon after they were married. The first of their eleven children, Elizabeth, was born on March 6, 1806, at Durham, England. Although the marriage seemed a happy one, Edward was basically selfish and never consulted with his family about his plans. He bought a large estate, Hope End, and spent considerable sums of borrowed money to improve it. It was a self-contained little paradise where Edward reigned supreme. They lived comfortably with income from sugar plantations worked by slaves in Jamaica.

As youngsters Elizabeth and her siblings enjoyed a happy, sheltered life. She was shy and very studious and was constantly reading or writing. Her father was so proud of her abilities that when she was twelve, he paid to have her epic poem, "The Battle of Marathon," printed. She later learned Greek, Latin, and several modern languages. She wanted to be first in everything—in cleverness, in goodness, and in being loved.

At fifteen Elizabeth fell and injured her spine and began to suffer weakness in her lungs. It is now thought that this was a form of tuberculosis with attacks brought on by nervous excitement. Her health was permanently damaged, although she was able to get about when she wished to. She wanted her own way and had begun to taste the power of invalidism, an escape route from household duties that gave her freedom to write. Her father let her read most of the books in his library. "Books and dreams were what I lived in." Here was a sturdy soul in a stunted body.

In 1828, when Elizabeth was twenty-two, her mother died, leaving a grief-stricken father. He now had the responsibility of bringing up eleven children alone. As the oldest, Elizabeth might have been expected to take over the running of the household, but the only duty she accepted was to teach the little boys the classics.

In 1831, facing financial ruin, Edward was forced to sell his beautiful home and later move to a dreary residence on Wimpole Street. This altered his way of life and personality. He kept his children in ignorance almost until the day they moved, although the servants had been whispering about it for some time. It seemed that by not speaking about anything unpleasant, Edward could persuade himself it had never happened. His emotional withdrawal first bewildered and then alienated the hearts and minds of his family.

Unpleasant scenes occurred as Edward made it clear that he would never allow any of his children to marry. If they did, they would be cut off from their inheritance. He began to treat his offspring like slaves. Indignant, Elizabeth determined to help her siblings and at times defied her father.

After two years of confinement in the fog and dampness of London, already weak from coughing, Elizabeth burst a blood vessel in her chest. Her doctor ordered her to go to the mild climate of the seashore at Torquay under the protection of an aunt, where she remained for three years.

Sisters and brothers came and went. She insisted that her favorite brother Edward, "Bro," remain with her. She said, "Father considered it to be very wrong in me to exact such a thing." In 1840 she was shocked and devastated over the drowning death of Bro and felt it was her fault.

Returning to London, wanting to obey her father, she became an invalid on the famous third floor at 50 Wimpole Street. In a dark room, forbidden exercise and air, she had only her books, correspondence, and poetry for occupation. She led a reclusive life but intellectually was very active. Her room was sealed up for the winter lest dust in the atmosphere irritate her lungs. A fire was kept burning day and night, and with little oxygen she grew weaker and weaker.

Elizabeth had a personal maid, Wilson, to attend her needs and her spaniel, Flush, as a companion. Her sister Arabel stayed with her at night. Elizabeth took opium to quiet her heart. At least she had a "room of her own"—essential for creativity. Isolation and inactivity were food for her poetry; yet at the age of thirty she had not yet published anything in her own name.

The first work issued under her name was *The Seraphim and Other Poems. The Seraphim* takes place at the time of the Crucifixion. The two seraphim speak of the Creation, Fall of man, birth of Christ—the Incarnation—and redemption.

Elizabeth never lost her simple orthodox Christian faith, and she read her Bible every day. All her life she remained untouched by evolutionary thought. She had a broad, generous, idealistic Christian point of view.

Every evening for four years her father would pray at her bedside "with one of my hands held in his and nobody besides him and me in the room." With little concept of love, he jealously dominated her life, even overseeing her food and medicine. She was completely devoted to him and seemed reasonably content with her life.

Elizabeth published a volume of poetry in 1838 and in 1844 a collection of poems dedicated to her father. These two books marked her as one of the principal women of letters in England. Her poetry brought her both popularity and critical acclaim.

One of those who admired her poems was the young poet Robert Browning, who began a correspondence with her in January 1845. In his first letter to her he wrote, "I love your verses with all my heart, dear Miss Barrett." Then after a page or two he added, "And I love you too."

When Robert Browning stormed into her life, Elizabeth was a thirty-nine-year-old invalid who thought she was dying and had already seen the best part of her life. She was six years older than Browning.

Robert Browning (1812-1889), one of the greatest poets of Victorian England, had never attended a university. He was educated through reading the classics in his father's library and by several tutors. His mother was a devout Christian and passed on to her son the foundations of her faith.

A literary career was determined for him in boyhood, and his early works were printed at the expense of Browning's family. He traveled a great deal and fell in love with Venice (if you've been there, you understand why). He declared, "Italy was my university." Ever afterwards he wanted to return to his "heart"—Italy.

His life was almost wholly given to his writing, dramatic monologues being among his finest works. With robust optimism he had faith in the value of human life and wrote:

> *God's in His Heaven,*
> *All's right with the world!*

It is ironic that the publication of the poems dedicated to her father brought Elizabeth the correspondence, later the visits, and the growing love of Robert Browning that ultimately released her from emotional servitude to her father. Browning's love was generous, just, mature, and unselfish compared to Edward's colossal selfishness. After an extended correspondence, Robert came to visit Elizabeth for the first time on May 20, 1845. They were soon deeply in love.

In the next sixteen months Robert was a regular visitor to Wimpole Street, but father and suitor never met. Edward was in the city during the daytime, and Robert always left before his return. Edward disliked being introduced to any of his children's friends, as he preferred to ignore their existence and convey his disapproval. Elizabeth wrote that he felt it his duty to rule like the kings of Christendom, by divine right, but she still believed he loved his children. In between visits Robert and Elizabeth exchanged letters almost daily.

During these months Elizabeth wrote the first draft of *Sonnets from the Portuguese*. (Robert often called her "my little Portuguese" because of her dark complexion.) In these forty-four sonnets she recorded her growing love for Browning. She wrote the sonnets in secret, never thinking of publication; nor did she show them to Robert until several years later. He then insisted that they belonged to the world and had them published. They are considered among the most eloquent love poems in the language, although sometimes overly sentimental.

> *"Guess now who holds thee?"*
> *"Death," I said. But there*
> *The silver answer rang, "Not Death,*
> *But love."*

> *If thou must love me, let it be for naught*
> *Except for love's sake only.*

> *How do I love thee? Let me count the ways,*
> *I love thee to the depth and breadth and height*
> *My soul can reach, when feeling out of sight . . .*
> *I love thee with the breath, smiles*
> *Tears of all my life!—And, if God choose,*
> *I shall but love thee better after death.*

With Robert's encouragement Elizabeth, or Ba, as she was called, walked up and down stairs and even out of doors during warm weather. They agreed to marry secretly at the end of the summer. Doctors said that Ba could not live through another cold, foggy London winter and urged her to go to Italy. However, her father refused to allow her to leave. On hearing of Edward's decision, Browning rushed out immediately and got a marriage license. They were secretly married on September 12, 1846, and within a week left for Italy, taking along her servant, Wilson, and her dog, Flush.

On the way to Pisa she received a terrible letter from her father. He disinherited her, considered her dead, and she never saw or heard from him again. After her elopement Edward said, "My daughter is now in her grave—let us forget the dead." The other two of his children who married in his lifetime, Henrietta and Alfred, were treated in exactly the same way.

An excellent play, *The Barretts of Wimpole Street* by Rudolf Besier, dramatized the courtship of Elizabeth and Robert, making them even more famous. This play had a long, successful run on Broadway. In 1934 a film was made of their romance, starring Norma Shearer, Frederic March, and Charles Laughton. It was a top box-office hit. Also the famous English author Virginia Woolf wrote *Flush, a Biography* about the Brownings.

Elizabeth had inherited money from relatives, which was fortunate, as Robert still had very little income. Because of the mild climate and lower cost of living, they settled at the Villa Casa Guidi in Florence, Italy.

Elizabeth's health improved remarkably, and although she continued to be a semi-invalid, Robert was constant in his love and tenderness. Their marriage of over fourteen years was supremely happy. Because of her physical weakness, she had trouble sleeping. She commented on that difficulty in the following verse:

> *Of all the thoughts of God that are*
> *Borne inward into souls afar,*
> *Along the Psalmist's music deep,*
> *Now tell me if that any is,*
> *For gift or grace, surpassing this:*
> *"He giveth His beloved—sleep?"*

The Brownings were never separated after their marriage except for a day or two, so there were no more letters. Elizabeth continued to write to her father asking for forgiveness, but he never responded nor allowed his children to mention her name. Eventually all her letters were returned unopened, and the packet was addressed to Robert. Edward said he regretted keeping them so long, through his ignorance of where he should send them. Elizabeth's brothers were also unkind, so she decided never to live in England again. She did correspond with her sisters Arabel and Henrietta.

The Brownings traveled about Italy, went to Paris where they met author George Sand, and visited London, hoping to see her father, but that did not happen. The only sorrow in her new life was that her father never forgave her although she had become very famous. She remained uncrushed by his rejection.

Elizabeth always felt at home in Florence where her son Pen was born when she was forty-three. She became interested in Italian politics and wrote a great deal of not very good poetry, such as *Casa Guidi Windows*, hoping for the unification of Italy. She also wrote *Aurora Leigh*, a novel in blank verse that was her most ambitious work. Someone has called it "a masterpiece in embryo," but she was never boastful or conceited about her work.

Because of their growing fame, Elizabeth and Robert had numerous visitors and were always gracious in their rich, full lives. They were acquainted with Wordsworth, Tennyson, the Hawthornes, Ruskin, Carlyle, Florence Nightingale, James Russell Lowell, and many others.

Elizabeth's health gave way when she was fifty-five. She died in Browning's arms and is buried in the old Protestant Cemetery in Florence. After her death Browning never returned to Florence, as he said his heart was buried there. He never remarried. His sister came to live with him in London where he gave his full time to writing. The Pre-Raphaelites William and Dante Gabriel Rossetti respected Browning and were aware of his greatness. In a sense Browning never lost his enthusiastic optimism. Here are a few well-known verses:

Open my heart and you will see
Graved inside of it, "Italy."

Oh, to be in England
Now that April's there.

The Year's at the Spring
And day's at the morn:
God's in His Heaven
All's right with the world.

Ah, but a man's reach should extend his grasp,
Or what's a Heaven for?

Every joy is gain
And gain is gain, however small.

What I call God
And fools call nature.

Grow old along with me!
The best is yet to be,
The last of life, for which the first was made,
Our times are in His hand.

In 1889 Robert Browning died in the home of his son Pen on the Grand Canal at the Palazzo Rezzorico in Venice. Elizabeth had died twenty-eight years earlier. (The glories of Venice drew another great man to the Grand Canal, Richard Wagner, who died in nearby Palazzo in 1883.) Browning is buried in Westminster Abbey.

Though Elizabeth's writings were more admired in her day than Robert's, his reputation is much greater today. The variety of Browning's interests and the impressive range of his work makes him one of England's most important poets. As for Elizabeth, she had a wide influence in her time and is considered one of the finest women poets of Victorian England.

BIBLIOGRAPHY
Browning, Elizabeth Barrett. *The Poetical Works.* New York: Worthington, 1890.

Browning, Robert. *Poems by Robert Browning.* London: Routledge & Sons, 1900.

Irvine, William and Park Honan. *The Book, the Ring, and the Poet: A Biography of Robert Browning.* New York: McGraw, 1974.

Taplin, Gardner B. *The Life of Elizabeth Barrett Browning.* New Haven, Conn.: Yale University Press, 1957

RECOMMENDED READING

Elizabeth Barrett Browning
>   *Poems,* 1844
>   *Sonnets from the Portuguese*
>   *Aurora Leigh*

Robert Browning
>   *Home Thoughts, from Abroad*
>   *Pippa Passes*
>   *My Last Duchess*

AMY CARMICHAEL

1867-1951

Nothing was impossible
to the God of the impossible.

Amy Carmichael

The great author, missionary, and founder of Dohnavur Fellowship, Amy Carmichael, was born in the seacoast village of Millisle, Northern Ireland. The oldest of seven children, she had leadership qualities at an early age, a fun-loving nature, and a rich imagination.

Her poetic nature was expressed in her love of color. "Blueness of sea that looked happy, grayness of sea that looked anxious, greenness of sea that looked angry—these are my first memories of color," she said. The Carmichaels were a happy, prosperous family brought up on the Bible and the Shorter Catechism.

Amy was deeply devoted to her mother, who often spoke to her about the love of Jesus Christ. However, Amy was not able to comprehend God's love until the age of fifteen when she attended a children's mission meeting. Here she heard the chorus "Jesus loves me—this I know, for the Bible tells me so," and finally she opened her heart to Christ and became a child of God.

When Amy's father died suddenly at the age of fifty-four, God had prepared Mrs. Carmichael with this verse from Scripture: "The Lord is good, a stronghold in the day of trouble; and He knows those who trust in Him" (Nahum 1:7 NKJV).

Amy, now seventeen, became her mother's great support. Because of financial difficulties, the family moved to Belfast where Amy started a Bible class for "shawlies"—girls who worked in factories and wore shawls instead of hats. This work, called "the Welcome," drew hundreds of women because Amy was a fine leader, full of enthusiasm and energy, and an excellent organizer—qualities so essential in her future work.

Once she asked an elderly wealthy man to help buy needed property. When he indignantly refused, she began looking to the Lord only for financial provision. She followed this principle the rest of her life.

The Keswick Convention, with its emphasis on deepening the spiritual life, had a profound influence on Amy. The teachings there, especially those of its founder Robert Wilson, whom she called the "Dear Old Man" (D.O.M. for short), prepared her for her life work in India. After the death of Wilson's wife and daughter, Amy became a daughter-companion, and she lived with the "D.O.M." for several years. Here she met great men of God such as Hudson Taylor, founder of the China Inland Mission, and F. B. Meyer, a remarkable preacher and the author of many helpful books.

In spite of the aching sorrow of leaving her family and the lonely "D.O.M.," she felt the call of God to go as a missionary to Japan. On the long sea voyage to the East, the ship's captain became a Christian upon seeing the reality of Christ in Amy's life.

While she was in Japan, a young man seems to have fallen in love with her, as she was not only beautiful outwardly but inwardly as well. She was anxious about the future, and Satan kept whispering, "You are going to be very lonely." After an agonizing day of prayer, she decided to remain single, holding on to God's promise, "None of them that trust in Me shall be desolate." Amy said, "That word has been with me ever since."

After fifteen strenuous months in Japan resulting in numerous conversions, her health deteriorated. Often overworked, she had developed neuralgia and severe headaches, to the point that she was forced to return to England, to her family and the "D.O.M." Yet she believed God had sent her for training to Japan for whatever lay ahead. Her letters from Japan were collected and published as her first book, *From Sunrise Land*, the beginning of a long series of books.

Certain of her call as a missionary, she left her comfortable life with family and friends again when she recovered her health. She was uncertain about India when she arrived there in November 1895. People whispered that her health would not last six months, but she remained there more than fifty-five years, until her death on January 18, 1951. She loved India as few have loved it and is buried at Dohnavur, South India.

Amy worked hard to learn an Indian language, Tamil, with Rev. Thomas Walker of Tinnevelly as her teacher, trusty guide, and adviser. She had great admiration for Walker and considered him one of the finest men ever sent as a missionary to India. Tamil did not come easily to her. Half whimsically and half seriously she said that the words of Numbers 22:28 brought comfort to her: "Then the Lord opened the mouth of the donkey" (NKJV). She had a delightful sense of humor and once said, "Isn't it good that missionaries can laugh together?"

Her motto was, "Nothing too precious for Jesus," and a favorite quote by Samuel Rutherford was, "There are some who would have Christ cheap. They would have Him without the cross, but the price will not come down."

At first Amy went about temple towns and villages as an evangelist with a group of women called "the starry cluster." They traveled by night to escape the crushing heat and were often in danger, as they were met with scorn and persecution. In Amy's words, it was "a little thing committed to the hand of God."

Persistent in seeking the lost, Amy looked to God for direction by reading the Bible continually and labored in prayer often to exhaustion. She especially treasured that wonderful little book *Daily Light*, a morning and evening collection of Bible verses for each day in the year. She made many comments about events in the margins.

Hinduism, one of the world's oldest religions, is mostly confined to India where it originated. The three chief gods are Siva the destroyer, Vishnu the preserver, and Brahma, who is neutral. The Hindus worship hundreds of other gods that represent different aspects of Brahma. They also worship various animals, especially the sacred cow, and as pantheists believe that God is everything and everything is God. Superstition is rampant. Many people are vegetarians, practice Yoga, and believe in reincarnation—that the soul passes from body to body until reunited with Brahma. The caste system is very rigid. There is no distinction between cruelty and noncruelty, no right nor wrong nor ultimate truth. One is never sure which god to worship, but certainly all these gods are dead. Hinduism is based on mythology. Christianity is grounded in historical fact. Only Christ has been raised from the dead, and He will return to rule the world.

One of the horrors of Hinduism in Amy's time was the selling of little girls and boys to "marry" the Brahman temple priests. These children were sexually exploited and early introduced to unspeakable practices. Amy discovered that the traffic in children was secretive, vicious, and widespread. Here was the darkness and cruelty of heathenism.

After Amy learned that temple scouts were in many places looking for babies to be trained by older women to serve the priests as prostitutes, she called it "deified sin." Often children were sold by their parents because of poverty.

On March 6, 1901, a child named Preena fled from the temple back to her mother. The mother let her be returned to the temple, and it was decided to "marry" Preena to one of the gods. Children brought up in temples were introduced to the vilest practices as slaves of the gods. Preena threw herself on the temple floor and asked to die. Amy Carmichael was able to rescue her in spite of great danger from supernatural demonic forces. Thus began Amy's life work of saving children in moral danger. Preena was Amy's faithful friend for forty-three years.

It took a long time to find this hidden traffic of children in temple towns, and at first it seemed almost impossible. Not for another three years was a second child rescued; then little by little more children began to arrive. From being evangelists, Amy and her coworkers became nursemaids.

Three of the first four children died, and Amy felt that all her hopes perished too. In years to come she kept the anniversary of that discouraging time as a day of prayer. Amy's whole work was based on prayer to the living God. She said, "When in doubt, pray, 'Thy will be done whatever that will may be.'"

Hard, difficult, exhausting years lay ahead for Amy and her helpers, as many children, already in poor health, died of dysentery and small-pox. However, "the family" steadily increased. There was no doctor nearby until Dr. May Powell arrived in 1924 and also Mabel Wade, an English nurse. Fellow missionaries were helpful as well.

Risks had to be taken in this lonely work—often they were in danger of arrest. False witnesses were just a matter of a few rupees (money bribes). Amy never intentionally broke the law, but she was often threatened in the battle to save the children. She was in danger of being sent to prison because of lawsuits by families of rescued children.

When feeling alone, Amy shared all her experiences with her heavenly Father, and the loneliness was expelled. With her intense love of God and awareness of evil and the work of Satan, she was fearless in her determination to save children from the horrors of temple life.

Her early book, *Things As They Are*, was rejected for publication because of its negative content. But later it was published and stirred thousands of shocked people to pray for India.

Determined that these *wanted* children should grow up in an atmosphere of love, Amy gradually developed a whole compound to house and educate them. She was guided to buy much land, and slowly, with a great deal of prayer, one building after another was constructed, including nurseries, schools, a house of prayer, a hospital, kitchens, and a farm. Gardens were planted to help feed the family, and cows were bought for milk. Because of Amy's love of beauty, things were orderly and handsomely done.

The boys' work began in 1918. God brought many fellow workers from various countries with a variety of gifts. As the leader (although Amy insisted that Christ was the invisible and true leader) Amy knew how to develop and use the gifts of others.

Dr. Murray Webb-Peploe took over the running of the hospital, and his brother Godfrey directed the boys' activities. Amy never asked others to do what she was not ready to do herself. She often worked beyond the limits of her strength, in spite of painful neuralgia, headaches, and poor eyesight. She seemed to be everywhere at once in the heat of the day or late at night caring for children.

It was a great joy and relief when her mother came to help for several months. But her mother, who had followed the work so closely through Amy's regular Dohnavur letters, died in 1913. Her loss was heartbreaking for Amy. Also, the death of Ponnammal, one of Amy's most loyal workers, from cancer in 1915 left a deep gap.

Finally in 1927, after many perilous adventures, Amy separated from the English mission and founded Dohnavur Fellowship. The object of the Fellowship was "to save children in moral danger; to train them to serve others; to succor the desolate and the suffering; to do anything that may be shown to be the will of our Heavenly Father, in order to make His love known, especially to the people of India."

Dohnavur is located in the country, not far from the Indian Ocean with beautiful mountains nearby. Just to look at them seemed to give Amy strength in times of exhaustion. The unifying cord in the Fellowship was the love of God and of each other in the midst of intense work and scorn from the outside world. Christ was made luminous in loving human lives.

In her wonderful book *Gold Cord*, Amy relates the story of the Fellowship. Assisting her in writing this book was Mrs. Phil Matthews, who later became a great patroness of L'Abri Fellowship.

It must be mentioned here that three great missionary works have had a profound influence on L'Abri Fellowship: the China Inland Mission founded by Hudson Taylor, George Muller's orphanages in England, and Dohnavur Fellowship. All four of these remarkable works are based on the truth of the Bible and prayer to the living God, who does supply our needs both spiritually and financially.

Amy's family (she was now called Amma—Tamil for Mother) grew into hundreds. As Amma said, "We grew up simply like a family of happy children." There was a lot of "holy drudgery," but wherever Amma was, there was happiness. She was imaginative and had a great sense of humor. She loved to play with the children, inventing games or telling little nature stories, and she was very gentle with the sick.

However, she was strict and would punish when necessary. She faced many trials, but she was a true mother protecting "her children." Amy read whenever time allowed and early learned to avoid careless talk about others. Although she never married, she encouraged and often helped arrange good marriages for her "family."

Forthright and careful about truth, she was concerned about unconverted people. The love of God within her was so powerful that others were irresistibly drawn to God. Never self-seeking, she gave God the glory.

Suddenly, on September 24, 1931, tragedy struck. At twilight Amy was examining a new building under construction, and she fell into a pit where no pit should have been. She broke several bones, and the pain was excruciating. For months the Fellowship prayed for healing, but God answered in a different way.

After a second fall in her room, she was virtually bedridden for the last twenty years of her life and rarely able to be taken about. All manner of health complications developed, and she was often in great pain with sleepless nights. But she was active in her mind and spirit.

Amy had seen thirty-six years of "the warfare of the service"—younger workers with strength and energy to do the hard work. Now twenty years "keeping of the charge"—older ones for prayer, godly wisdom, and vision. The inscription over her door was "the room of peace."

From her bed of pain and prayer, she continued to direct the Fellowship, although longing to relinquish the burden. She was deeply loved and cared for. Among those who faithfully watched over her were Mary Mills (Amma called her the perfect nurse), Neela—Amma's secretary and right-hand helper, and Aurlai, who was rescued as a child of eleven and served with Amma for forty years.

During both world wars as the pound devalued, there was a great deal of struggle and prayer for survival at Dohnavur Fellowship. The family slowly grew to over 900.

In her last years only the most serious problems were brought to Amma, and when she was well enough, children were brought to visit her, and prayer meetings were held in her room. However, she kept in touch with many through her letters, sometimes referred to as "prison letters" (reminding one of Paul). She never lost her faith in God's love and mercy.

Through these years, in spite of great pain, poor eyesight, and often in an uncomfortable position, she wrote some of her finest books, hymns, and poetry. She knew how to write in a way to comfort the suffering. There is a deep mysticism in her writing. In all she wrote thirty-five books, some short and some longer. *From Sunrise Land* was her first, and *This One Thing* her last. These handsome books are bound in blue, her favorite color, and often contain beautiful pictures. Her writings have gone into many translations and some as well into Braille, and continue to be widely read.

Many of her poems are set to music in the hymnbook *Wings* and are still sung at Dohnavur. Amma believed music to be the language of heaven.

Amy Carmichael died peacefully in her sleep at the age of eighty-four. Now she was safe at home forever. As her coworker Barbara Osman said, "It was a day marked by beauty and order." Amma's grave is distinguished by a beautiful stone birdbath erected beside it, for birds often reminded her of God's love.

Dohnavur Fellowship continues under the spiritual leadership of Jesus Christ, and among those the Fellowship prays for is L'Abri Fellowship. Various of their workers have visited Swiss L'Abri.

Each of us in our lives leaves a parade of influence behind us. Amma's parade is magnificent.

BIBLIOGRAPHY

Houghton, Frank. *Amy Carmichael of Dohnavur*. London: S.P.C.K., 1955.

RECOMMENDED READING

Things as They Are
Lotus Buds
Ponnammal
Nor Scrip
Gold Cord
Ploughed Under
Gold by Moonlight
Figures of the True
Though the Mountains Shake
This One Thing
Wings (with music)

WILLA CATHER

1873-1947

The universal human yearning for something permanent,
enduring, without shadow of change.

Willa Cather in
Death Comes to the Archbishop

W illa Cather, one of America's finest women novelists, was interested as a child in the medical profession because of her friendship with local doctors. Later while studying at the University of Nebraska, one of her essays was published and received enthusiastic praise. After seeing her name in print, she decided that writing was to be her whole life. In spite of many hardships and years of poverty, she never swerved from this determination. Deeply absorbed in her work, she remained single and cherished the necessary solitude and freedom to write. But while Willa Cather had her solitude, she also had a large family and numerous friends. For over forty years Edith Lewis, whom she first met in Lincoln in 1903, was her helpful companion.

Others have chosen a similar path for the sake of their art. For example, Jane Austen, the Brontë sisters, Christina Rossetti, Emily Dickinson, Mary Cassatt, Michelangelo, Handel, Brahms, Beethoven, Schubert, and so on. Singleness of purpose does not mean that one has to be lonely, although there must be many, many hours of aloneness.

Willa was born in the lovely Shenandoah Valley of northern Virginia near Winchester, where much of the Civil War had raged. When she was three, her family moved to a sheep farm, Willowshade, not far from the village of Back Creek. In early years, Willie (her nickname) was home-schooled by her Grandmother Boak, a lady of culture and intellect. There was a strong evangelical influence in the family.

Willa's mother and grandmother were well-read in the Bible and the classics, especially Shakespeare and *Pilgrim's Progress*. As a child, Willie read *Pilgrim's Progress* out loud to her two grandmothers eight times. Loving to read, Willa began to collect her own books and marked them "The Private Library of Wm. Cather, Jr." Number one was the Bible.

At the age of nine she was uprooted from her beautiful, comfortable home in Virginia when her family moved to a prairie farm in Nebraska. It was a shattering experience, and though she eventually came to love Nebraska, she never forgot the trauma of her transplantation. Remembering the gentle hills and valleys of Virginia, she referred to Nebraska as "a country as bare as a piece of sheet iron."

The Divide, a stretch of plain and prairie north of Red Cloud, was lonely with hard nature to combat, but Willa had a high regard for the courage and industry of the pioneers. She spent her childhood among immigrant farmers and through them learned to love the land. Farm talk was a frequent subject of conversation at home.

This harsh countryside later provided her with the setting and characters for much of her finest work. She commented, "The years from eight to fifteen are the formative period in a writer's life when he or she unconsciously gathers basic material." Willie forgot nothing of her growing-up years and used a large amount of autobiographical material in her poems, short stories, and novels.

Willa's mother, Jennie, was strict and demanding and, when she thought it necessary, disciplined her children with a rawhide whip. Willa's gentle, tenderhearted father was so kind that he made little leather shoes for his favorite sheepdog so she wouldn't cut her feet on the rocks in the pasture.

The Cathers were poor, and when they moved to the nearby town of Red Cloud, there was little privacy, as the large family was packed into a small rented house. Willa, the oldest of seven children, shared a tiny attic room with her favorite brothers, Douglas and Roscoe.

There was little leisure in this busy household, but every free moment Willa climbed to the attic and read all kinds of books with unsparing industry. This too prepared her for her later work. She dressed as a tomboy and was a rebel. Older people interested her, especially men who had ideas and searching minds.

A notable influence on her studies was the Englishman William Ducker, a local clerk who helped her to read Latin and Greek when she was thirteen. She believed he also taught her to think. She learned too from the intellectual melting pot of immigrant European pioneers in this dusty prairie town—growing up a child of genius.

With strong likes and dislikes, Willa did not care for her public schoolteachers and only received about two years of public schooling before attending the University of Nebraska. She entered the school on borrowed money, knowing how hard and humiliating poverty can be.

In spite of a heavy schedule, she worked as a newspaper columnist and theater critic to earn money. She also edited the school magazine, *The Hesperian*, which included many of her early stories. Leading a spartan life, and with a great aptitude for study, she was considered the most brilliant student ever to graduate from the university. In her commencement speech she said, "There is another book of God than that of scriptural revelation—a book written in the chapters of creation upon the pages of the universe bound in mystery."

In her excellent book, *Willa Cather Living*, Edith Lewis describes Willa as having a slim figure, curling chestnut brown hair, and fair skin. What was most interesting about her were her eyes. "They were dark blue eyes, with dark lashes; and I know of no way of describing them, except to say they were eyes of genius. I have never met any gifted person who did not have extraordinary eyes."

After graduation Willa began work as a newspaperwoman in Pittsburgh. She lived in a cheap boarding house with miserable food, and she sent as much money as she could to her family in Red Cloud. These were her hardest years because she was homesick, but she knew she could not go back to Nebraska, as she felt it was both the happiness and the curse of her life.

In 1900 she left newspaper journalism and taught English for several years in Allegheny, Pennsylvania, in order to have three months' leisure to develop her writing. Attending the theater one night, she met tall, handsome Isabelle McClung, who became her lifelong friend. Isabelle invited Willa to live in her spacious family home where Willa enjoyed tranquillity and physical comfort she had never experienced before. In a small room at the top of the house, Willa wrote most of the short stories of her first book, *The Troll Garden*, and part of *April Twilights*, a volume of poems.

In 1902 Willa and Isabelle made their first trip abroad, which was a great imaginative experience. In order to help cover expenses Willa wrote charming essays describing their travels for an American newspaper. These are available in *Willa Cather in Europe*. Among them is a description of her famous meeting with poet A. E. Housman. These essays give valuable insight into her writing style, especially the influence of Flaubert, Maupassant, and Daudet.

In later life she traveled extensively, especially to France—a favorite city was Avignon. The impact of the Old World on the New World is a dominating theme in Willa Cather's writing.

In 1906 she joined the staff of *McClure's Magazine* in New York. Now thirty-two, she was already seasoned in dealing with words and soon became editor of this prominent literary magazine. One of her most poignant short stories, "Paul's Case," was published in it.

S. S. McClure and Willa were a good team, respecting each other's abilities. McClure once said, "Never discourage talent. Discouragement hurts talent far more often than it helps." McClure certainly encouraged Willa, but in her stressful responsibilities as editor, she had little time for her own writing.

A lasting influence on Willa's life was her friend, the author Sarah Orne Jewett, who wrote to Willa: "You must find your own quiet center of life and write from that to the world . . . to work in silence and with all one's heart, that is the writer's lot; he is the only artist who must be solitary, and yet needs the widest outlook upon the world." On this advice Willa took the courageous step of resigning from *McClure's* in 1912 and left behind financial security. At nearly forty, relatively late in her career, she devoted herself to her own fiction and style of writing.

Jewett urged Cather to take a simple rural subject that she knew well and write about it. This advice resulted in her superb prairie novels, *O Pioneers* (1913), *The Song of the Lark* (1915), and *My Ántonia* (1918). In them Cather created strong female characters who have courage, hope, and dignity. She depicts both the challenges and the splendor of life, for she wanted life to have splendor. These novels met with such success that she was able to live on the income from her books until her death in 1947.

O Pioneers is the heroic story of a young Swedish immigrant, Alexandra Bergson, who works hard to raise a successful farm out of the barren Nebraska plain. In one terrible scene Alexandra's favorite brother, Emil, is found with Marie, a married woman, and they are murdered by her husband. There is an inexpressible sadness in Cather's work. Even when she is describing life's terrors, she always insists on its beauties— the dream is still there; we just can't have it.

With her lyrical gift of speech and magnificent poetic prose, Cather had a genius for expression. A favorite quote from *O Pioneers* is: "I like trees because they seem more resigned to the way they have to live than other things do."

The Song of the Lark, her longest work, is a novel of great power and richness. There are many passionate scenes, but the passion is about Thea's life work, not her love life. Thea Kronberg, daughter of a Swedish Methodist minister, lives in poverty in Moonstone, Colorado. After years of struggle, she escapes from Moonstone and becomes a famous opera singer. Moonstone is in reality Red Cloud with its stuffy conventions and petty jealousies—"The fear of the tongue, that terror of little towns." Three men befriend her and help her to break from grinding poverty.

Thea, one of Willa's noble, independent women, is an assimilation of the great Wagnerian opera singer Olive Fremstad (a friend of Willa's) and of Willa herself. She was wise to write about what she knew from personal experience. Brilliant light pervades this novel, a radiance none of her other books evoke.

Thea loved the bright solitude of the desert sun and sand; sun filled her being for months on end. Even in Denver, Chicago, and New York there are blazing sunsets, stars sparkling like diamonds, and snow glistening with the shining moon.

Although Willa took great pleasure in writing *The Song of the Lark*, she was inclined to be critical of it because of her interest in music. In a later edition she deleted much wordiness. The first part of this novel is the most intriguing, as success is never so interesting as the struggle to attain it. *Song* is the unforgettable work of a vigorous, original talent.

Willa Cather was not trained as a musician, but music was vital in her life. While she worked as a reporter on the Pittsburgh newspaper, her desk was next to the music critic's. They had long conversations, and she never lost her intense interest and love of great music. *The Song of the Lark, One of Ours, My Mortal Enemy, Lucy Gayheart*, and various short stories include musical themes. Music had a strong influence on her imaginative process. She attended operas and concerts throughout her writing career.

The third of her prairie novels is the wonderful book *My Ántonia*. In a nostalgic folktale style, it describes the heroic struggle of a young Czech girl and her family to overcome poverty and the cold barrenness of the prairie with its droughts, blizzards, hail storms, and prairie fires. "Winter lies too long in country towns; hangs on until it is stale and sloppy, old and sullen," she writes.

One of Cather's favorite quotes from this book is: *"Optima dies . . . prima fuget"*—"The best days are the first to flee." Even so, *My Ántonia* has a happy ending because of Cather's affirmation of life.

Considered one of the finest short novels in American literature, *A Lost Lady* is what Willa called the "novel *demeublé*"—that is, writing "without extra furniture." She felt that novels had become too heavy and complex because of the writings of George Eliot.

Willa had a firm conviction that "art should simplify." She early chose a strong, simple style—similar to Gertrude Stein's, whose call was to "simplify, simplify, simplify," and to Emily Dickinson's startling brief poems. *A Lost Lady* is the story of a beautiful woman, Mrs. Forrester, whose wealthy husband becomes ill and is confined to a wheelchair. A young man, Niel, platonically loves and admires Mrs. Forrester but is disillusioned when she has an affair with a guest.

The past was important to Willa Cather, and she worked more with memory than invention. She said, "Life began for me when I ceased to admire and began to remember." Again she said, "A book is made with one's own flesh and blood of years . . . it is cremated youth." Yet for her, writing was sport, recreation. She never sat down with just a sense of duty, for she became so engrossed in her writing that she forgot any personal problems she might have had. What she needed was time and quiet to perfect her work.

Willa Cather approached her writing with intense pleasure and employed a technique similar to improvisation in playing music—she filled in details as inspiration came but worked with a firm underlying design. She wrote her first draft with great speed, working generally two or three hours each morning. Then with concentrated application, she rewrote the whole story on her typewriter, adding and subtracting as she went along. She was always very painstaking about her facts. Then her secretary typed a copy in which Cather made further changes and corrections. (Rewriting is often an author's special pleasure.) With the help of Edith Lewis, she then carefully corrected all proofs before final publication.

Willa Cather believed that art and religion have a common inner source. She was brought up a Baptist with a love of the Bible and *Pilgrim's Progress*. In 1922, at the age of fifty, along with her parents she was confirmed in the Protestant Episcopal church. In this church there was no conflict between religion and art.

Her two Catholic books, *Death Comes for the Archbishop* (1927)—considered her best and most popular work—and *Shadows on the Rock* (1931), about Quebec, Canada, deal with the impact of the Old World on the New World. Although Willa was not a Catholic, she was very thankful for the warm reception of these books by the Catholic community.

Next to writing her novels, Cather's choice of Alfred Knopf as her publisher was the most important influence on her career. Not only did she achieve financial security, but Knopf gave her freedom to write as she chose. Knopf protected her in every way he could from outside pressures and let the world in general know of his great admiration for her and belief in her.

In her last novel, *Sapphira and the Slave Girl*, Cather returned to her Virginia roots. She must have had in mind memories of her own parents as she wrote about the death of Father and Mother in the story, but other than that, her early family life is not reflected in the book. However, Willa always said that it was what she left out that counted. If there was too much of anything, she was eager to cut it out. Set before the Civil War, the book is a novel without a heroine, written in an austere style, of a time that will never return.

A close friend said about Willa, "I have never met anyone at all like her." In her notoriety Willa met many famous people, but she always remained loyal to her close friends, never acted "the celebrity," and was humble about her work. She believed intensely in the artist's right to a private life, especially as her books became more and more widely read. Her will prohibited any of her letters to be published—what a pity!—as apparently she was an excellent correspondent as well as a vivid conversationalist.

Because of her creativity, wonderful balance, and genuineness, she received honorary degrees and won the Pulitzer Prize for *One of Ours*. She was the first woman to receive an honorary degree from Princeton University.

The contemplation of death has central place in Cather's work. "The hard road of life with its penalties and punishments, and then always the inevitable end was one of her great themes." To her it seemed that the world broke apart as America turned to materialism. She struggled over the meaning of life and grew continually more pessimistic. Her tendency to look to the past increased with the years and was not helpful to her art. She was attacked by left-wing critics for being old-fashioned, even though she remained one of America's best loved and widely read authors.

Because of her poor health, work was nearly impossible in the last seven years of her life. Living on Park Avenue, she was not a recluse, but her activities were limited. During these years one of her greatest pleasures was her friendship with the amazing Menuhin family. One of the children, Yehudi, is today a world-renowned violinist.

Willa Cather died on a sunlit April day and is buried at Jaffrey, New Hampshire, where for years she spent summers at the Shattuck Inn. Seeking solitude, she often wrote in a tent set up in nearby woods. She never cared for luxury.

She had a restrained and beautiful style of writing, with a sense of dignity, timelessness, and virtue. Her books are wholesome with strong moral values. A sturdy traditionalist, yet original, with warmth of character, Willa Cather possessed a remarkable creative force.

BIBLIOGRAPHY

Brown, E. K. *Willa Cather: A Critical Biography*. New York: Alfred A. Knopf, 1953.

Lewis, Edith. *Willa Cather Living*. New York: Alfred A. Knopf, 1953.

RECOMMENDED READING

O Pioneers
The Song of the Lark
My Ántonia
One of Ours
A Lost Lady
My Mortal Enemy
Death Comes for the Archbishop
Shadows on the Rock
Lucy Gayheart
Sapphira and the Slave Girl
Short Stories

EMILY DICKINSON

1830-1886

There is no Frigate like a Book
To take us Lands away,
Nor any coursers like a Page
Of prancing Poetry.

Emily Dickinson

The two greatest women poets of the nineteenth century, Emily Dickinson and Christina Rossetti, were born the same year within a few days of each other. Their lives were amazingly similar outwardly. Both were abnormally reserved, both loved deeply but never married, and both withdrew from the world. However, they were decidedly different in expressing their frustrations and resignations.

Christina Rossetti wrote as a devout Anglican and acknowledged God in all her work throughout her life. Emily Dickinson struggled with her "Puritan" upbringing and to an extent challenged the Deity. Rossetti's tone is melancholy, while Dickinson's is sharp and introspective. Rossetti's verse is formal and traditional, while Dickinson's is experimental, "reckless in rhyme and audacious in idiom" (Louis Untermeyer).

Although the whole truth about Emily will elude us, we can better understand this strange, original genius, whose greatest poems are like jewels, by considering some of the details of her life.

The second of three children, she was born in Amherst, Massachusetts, where she lived most of her fifty-six years. She was close to her brother Austin, whose role was to lift her spirits. When he was away in Boston, she missed him and urged him to come home; so finally he settled with his wife, Susan, next door.

The two passions of Emily's sister Lavinia were cats and Emily. In this close-knit family their father, Edward Dickinson, ruled supreme. The children were in awe and fear of him.

Edward Dickinson was described as thin, dry, and speechless. A lawyer, vigorous in duty and a good citizen, eventually becoming treasurer of Amherst College, he ruled his household despotically. The law came first. As Emily said of her father, he was "too busy with briefs to notice what we do."

Self-righteous and unimaginative, he wished his children to read only the Bible. He was a stern Calvinist and insisted that his family attend the Congregational church. Even though Emily never became a church member, she attended meetings regularly, at least until the age of twenty-five. She was nurtured in Puritan orthodoxy.

Although deeply attached to her family (there were many relatives), Emily said, "I never had a mother." Mrs. Dickinson was a shadowy figure, possibly broken by her husband's harshness, and eventually she became an invalid taken care of by Emily and Vinnie.

At the age of ten, Emily was enrolled at Amherst Academy and was happy in her seven years there. She had excellent teachers, especially Edward Hitchcock, a man of God and a man of science, who inspired his pupils with a love for nature, especially minerals and flowers. Emily was considered the Amherst wit and participated freely in student activities.

She attended Mount Holyoke, with its intense evangelical atmosphere, for two terms. With all her heart, Emily wanted to be a Christian, but her religious anxieties came early and were deep. At Mount Holyoke she discovered she could not share the religious life of her generation and their understanding of truth. She said, "I am continually putting off becoming a Christian." Concerning her family, she wrote, "They are religious—except me." Because of her severe, demanding father, it was hard for her to picture a loving heavenly Father. Even her ancestors were rigid Calvinists, but she had a quiet, rebellious personality.

Because of her poor health, Emily's father withdrew her from Mount

Holyoke when she was eighteen. That was the end of her formal education. From then on she educated herself by extensive reading. "Though largely self-taught, she was well taught." "The strongest friends of the soul—books."

The book she knew best was the Bible, which she read often and with enjoyment, especially the book of Revelation. She was saturated with Scripture and could summon verses at will, although she seldom quoted them exactly. Her fascination with words began when she was eleven, and she was a devoted student of Webster's dictionary. "The dictionary was the Bible of her religion, which was poetry" (Henry Wells). It is interesting that Noah Webster lived for a time in Amherst.

Emily Dickinson's favorite writer was Shakespeare, which tells us a lot. Like Shakespeare, she had a vast vocabulary. Then there was "dear Dickens"—her regard for him never waned to the end of her life. She also loved George Eliot's works and was intensely interested in the Brontës, especially in the poems of Emily Brontë. Influenced too by Elizabeth Barrett Browning, Emily decided that her business was to "love and sing"—that is, to be a poet.

For most of her life Emily lived in an Amherst mansion, the Homestead, that lacked many conveniences. Housekeeping was an incessant burden on the women of the family although they had servants. The household was run to suit her father. Not a domestic spirit, Emily learned to do her part, like Emily Brontë: "She makes all the bread for her father who only likes hers."

Her sister Vinnie took over the grosser tasks, as she was vigorous in protecting Emily. Vinnie adored Emily but never understood her greatness; nor did any of the family. Vinnie's love for cats brought out the comic spirit in Emily, who said, ". . . Vinnie with her pussies, for which Emily is seeking assassins." And she faulted the hens for not providing the wherewithal to make ice cream. "We have at present one cat and twenty-four hens, who do nothing so vulgar as lay an egg, which checks the ice cream tendency."

The Homestead became Emily's refuge *and* prison. Yet she did leave on occasion. While their father was a United States Congressman, Emily, then in her twenties, and Vinnie visited Washington in 1855. On their way home, the sisters stayed briefly with friends in Philadelphia. Here she heard the forty-one-year-old Presbyterian clergyman Charles Wadsworth preach, and it seems she fell in love with him. A poet in early life, he was happily married and at the height of his power as a preacher. There was no love affair with Wadsworth in the ordinary sense, as they only met several times, but she dedicated herself to the man's spirit.

According to theory, he had a profound influence on Emily as her muse and the inspiration of her greatest love poems. In correspondence with Wadsworth, Emily called him "My dearest earthly friend" and probably suffered the torments of undeclared love. Most likely he did not know of her profound emotions. After this painful experience, her poetry became increasingly mystical.

There is mystery here because Emily at eighteen had been influenced by B. F. Newton, a lawyer in her father's office. He visited in her home at various times and in 1850 introduced her to the poems of Emerson. She called him her Preceptor (teacher) and said he taught her immortality. Of her young friends, Newton, an ardent reader and thinker, was the only one who recognized her poetic promise. He said to her, "All can write autographs but few paragraphs; for we are mostly no more than names."

Three years later Newton married an older woman, and two years afterwards he died of tuberculosis. The news of his death was distressing to Emily.

> *My life closed twice before its close;*
> *It yet remains to see*
> *If Immortality unveil*
> *A third event to me,*
> *So huge, so hopeless to conceive,*
> *As these that twice befell.*
> *Parting is all we know of heaven,*
> *And all we need of hell.*

Emily's love poems are among the finest ever written by a woman.

Basically reticent, at the age of twenty she was already reluctant to see strangers. She worked hard for her keep and often resented the housework, especially when Vinnie was away. "She chose not to be yielded up to matrimony" or lose her freedom to the "prickly art of housekeeping."

In order to fit in the writing, which meant everything to her, she gradually gave up all activity either of a social or of a charitable nature outside the Homestead. She finally stopped visiting, using the excuse, "But Father objects because he is in the habit of me."

Though she did not escape her home in the flesh, she did so in her mind. Increasingly she lived in the freedom of imagination. "Her home was the setting, with a family that learned not to intrude. Her companions were her lexicon, the things of nature, her books, her letters . . . her poems . . ." (Richard Sewall).

Vinnie said that Emily was a very busy person—she had to think. Emily was "the only one of us" who had that to do. Vinnie explained, "Father believed; and Mother loved; and Austin had Amherst [College]; and I had the family to keep track of."

Emily gradually became a recluse and rarely went out except into the garden. An expert botanist and a careful observer of nature, she worked long and lovingly. Birds have always been the darlings of poets. She loved birds, especially the blue jay.

> *A bird came down the Walk;*
> *He did not know I saw;*
> *He bit an angle-worm in halves*
> *And ate the fellow, raw.*

> *The morns are meeker than they were,*
> *The nuts are getting brown;*
> *The berry's cheek is plumper,*
> *The rose is out of town.*

When visitors came to the Dickinson home, they saw only a figure vanishing down the hallway like a ghost. Emily always wore white and refused to be fitted for her clothes. She communicated with friends through many extraordinary letters but had others address her envelopes. She would often enclose poems, as the unfailing constant of her life was poetry.

Unfortunately only about a tenth of these letters still exist. Her niece, Martha Bianchi, collected some of them in *Life and Letters of Emily Dickinson*. A writer of great originality, some of Emily's most vivid expressions are found in her letters. Here is a sample: "If I read a book and it makes my whole body so cold no fire can ever warm me, I know that is poetry. If I feel physically as if the top of my head were taken off, I know that is poetry. These are the only ways I know it. Is there any other way?"

One of the important relationships of Emily's life was with Samuel Bowles—a special friend of Austin and Sue—whom she met about 1858. Bowles, a Unitarian, was an editor and publisher who enjoyed the platonic friendship of women, although he was a happily married man. Thirty-five of Emily's letters to Bowles survive, and nearly fifty poems were included. She was deeply in love with him for several years and never ceased loving him at a distance for the rest of her life. Her ill-starred love must have been desperate. She also hoped he would publish her poems.

Bowles referred to her as "Queen Recluse." He only bothered to publish five of her poems, all anonymously with manufactured titles (Emily rarely gave titles to her poems) and petty alterations.

Withdrawing more and more, Emily decided she would live only for her writing, that as a poet she would find the fulfillment she had missed as a woman. Two-thirds of Emily's poetry was written in the inspired, almost frenzied years between 1858 and 1865. At her peak she wrote a poem almost every day.

"Storm, wind, the wild March sky, sunsets and dawns, the birds and bees, butterflies and flowers of her garden, with a few trusted human friends, were sufficient companionship" (Mabel Loomis Todd, a friend of Emily's).

"Poetry was her playmate in years of loneliness, and she came to it with a sparkle in her eye and mischief on her lips" (George Whicher). Her secluded life was a veritable hothouse for breeding emotions. She lived in a world of fancy.

Emily experienced extreme depression, fear, anguish, numbness, despair, and she explored the desert places of the human heart. Her universe was the soul, resulting in gemlike verse resembling nothing written before or after. No major poet ever lived so private an existence, but she probably could not have written her poems without seclusion. After this prolific period, she had a nervous breakdown.

Christianity gave meaning to Emily's life in spite of her many questions and doubts. She suffered from her father's hyper-Calvinism and its legalism that goes beyond the Scriptures. She chose her words carefully in her writing and quoted the Bible most often in a Calvinistic framework. Some have called her Jonathan Edwards's enlightened successor.

Jonathan Edwards (1703-1758) had lived only seven miles from Emily's home. An American Congregational clergyman, Edwards preached Calvinistic doctrines of absolute divine sovereignty and human depravity. His sermons have possibly never been equaled for passionate strength and beauty of form. His sermon "Sinners in the Hands of an Angry God" was a key factor bringing America's Great Awakening. Heaven and hell were an urgent reality to Edwards. He is considered a great architect of the American mind.

Emily found it difficult to accept the Puritan God and was torn between her father's Christian faith and Emerson's transcendentalism. Religion haunted her rather than consoled her, as her relationship with God was ambiguous. She was caught in a conflict between faith and doubt because she had the skepticism of the transcendentalist. She argued that God plays hide-and-seek with His creatures, and she revolted against harsh Calvinism, becoming more and more mystical.

> *Some keep the Sabbath going to church;*
> *I keep it staying at home,*
> *With a bobolink for a chorister,*
> *And an orchard for a dome.*

She never forgot the God of her childhood and felt guilty over her religious struggles. In an early letter to Abiah Root she wrote, "I feel that I shall never be happy without I love Christ." Emily mistakenly thought she had to give up the world to become a Christian. "Let Emily sing for you because she cannot pray." She knew more about religion than anything other than literature. Some think that at heart she accepted orthodox doctrine. In spite of her questioning she wrote the following:

> *Given in marriage unto thee,*
> *Oh, thou celestial host.*
> *Bride of the Father and the Son*
> *Bride of the Holy Ghost.*
> *Other betrothal shall dissolve—*
> *Wedlock of will, decay—*
> *Only the keeper of this ring*
> *Conquers mortality.*

Her identification with the suffering Christ in her poetry is frequent and impressive.

Emily copied the following poem on the back leaf of her Bible:

The Bible

> *'Tis a pure and holy word,*
> *'Tis the wisdom of a God,*
> *'Tis a fountain full and free,*
> *'Tis the Book for you and me.*
> *'Twill the soul's best anchor be*
> *Over life's tempestuous sea,*
> *A guardian angel to the tomb,*
> *A meteor in the world's dark gloom;*
> *'Tis a shining sun at even,*
> *'Tis a diamond dropt from heaven.*

Another prominent man in Emily's life was the radical Unitarian minister Col. Higginson, with whom she corresponded for twenty-four years, until just before her death. She always needed an object or person on whom she could focus her creative powers. In writing to him, she signed herself "Your Scholar" and wanted to know his opinion of her poems.

Emily and Higginson only met twice in person. After the first meeting with her, Higginson said that he was glad not to live near her and confessed he had never been with anyone "who drained my nerve power so much." Sad to say, Emily never achieved a wholly satisfying relationship with anyone she had to be near. She demanded too much of people.

Higginson really did not understand Emily's greatness, and he altered her poems to make them more "normal," which may be one reason why she refused to be published. She never took anyone's advice about her writing because she knew the worth of her poetry.

In a letter to Higginson she wrote, "How do most people live without any thoughts?" "I find ecstasy in living—the mere sense of living is joy enough." Emily's poems show how sensitive she was to both the ecstasy and anguish of everyday experience. She lived through the trauma of the Civil War and yet does not refer to this in her poetry even though she despised slavery.

She delighted in her garden and the changing seasons. The events mirrored in her poetry lie in the experience of a sheltered woman moving from kitchen to drawing room to her upstairs desk and to the garden in a New England village. In this limited environment she wrote her "letter to the world" but failed to mail it herself.

> *This is my letter to the world*
> *That never wrote to me.*

Emily Dickinson continues to fascinate artistic people. Aaron Copland's most important work for voice and piano is his musical setting of twelve of Emily's poems. One of Martha Graham's greatest choreographic works for the theater is *Letter to the World*. A masterpiece, it chronicles the spiritual progress of Emily Dickinson from youth to her encounter with love and then to the realization that that love was forbidden. (When traveling on the New York subway to study modern dance with Martha Graham, Jane Stuart Smith often read Emily Dickinson.)

Emily had not only a piercing sense of beauty but also a delightful sense of humor with a leaning to satire. She commented, "Women talk; men are silent; that is why I dread women." However, she had special friends such as the Hollands, Helen Hunt Jackson, and Martha Loomis Todd. She was unselfish in caring for her mother and others. She wrote:

> *If I can stop one Heart from breaking*
> *I shall not live in vain*
> *If I can ease one Life the Aching*
> *Or cool one Pain*
> *Or help one fainting Robin*
> *Unto his Nest again*
> *I shall not live in Vain.*

After the sudden death of her father in 1874 while he was on a trip to Boston, Emily went deeper into seclusion and became known as "The Nun of Amherst." Others called her "the myth"—considering her eccentric. But she had contact with her family and close friends and was an avid newspaper reader. Yet in all her relationships she felt the threat of invasion of privacy, without which she could not function. "Creativity sometimes swallows you up," she wrote.

It seems she came to love her father's friend, Judge Lord, who was eighteen years older than herself. After his wife died, he found companionship with Emily and delighted in their conversations, especially concerning Shakespeare. Emily referred to these times as "Adventures in Literature." She rejoiced in the sheer thrill of words. When Judge Lord proposed marriage, she refused because she prized her liberty more than becoming the wife of a public man.

After Judge Lord's death in 1884, Emily suffered a nervous breakdown and was a semi-invalid for the rest of her life. Until the end, she continued writing poetry and letters. Some of her last poems were among her best and reveal her as a woman of high personal courage. One of her last letters was to a friend whose husband had just died: "'Eye hath not seen nor ear heard . . . ' What a recompense! The enthusiasm of God at the reception of His sons and daughters! How ecstatic! How infinite! Says the blissful voice, not yet a voice, but a vision: 'I will not let thee go, except I bless thee.'"

Emily Dickinson died of Bright's disease in the home where she was born, virtually unknown in her lifetime and unrecognized even by her family. She left her poems to her sister Vinnie.

> *Success is counted sweetest*
> *By those who ne'er succeed.*

Higginson read a poem by Emily Brontë at her funeral, "No coward soul is mine."

Vinnie found Emily's poems in a chaotic state hidden in boxes and bureau drawers, many written on margins of newspapers, brown paper bags, and backs of envelopes, or collected in little volumes tied together with twine. The handwriting was extremely difficult to read. In all Emily wrote nearly 1,800 poems.

Vinnie kept pushing for publication. She really did not understand her sister's poetry but believed Emily was a shining genius. Emily had not allowed her poems to be published during her life as, being far ahead of her time, she could not believe she would gain a hearing and knew criticism would be unhelpful.

Emily's close friends, Col. Higginson and Mabel Loomis Todd, edited and arranged for the publication of the first edition of her poems three years after her death in 1890. Vinnie helped to pay for the printing of 480 copies, which sold remarkably well. At last Emily's "Letter to the World" had been sent out.

Her poems were divided into four groups—Life, Nature, Love, Time and Eternity. Many of them dealt with her obsession about death and immortality.

> *Because I could not stop for Death,*
> *He kindly stopped for me;*
> *The carriage held but just ourselves*
> *And immortality.*

Emily's writings were influenced by the Bible, Protestant hymns, Shakespeare, and Emerson. She often used a simple four-line stanza such as those found in the hymns of Isaac Watts, writing in this orthodox form to express unorthodox views.

Unconventional, she was accused of poetic chaos, lack of rhyme, and poor grammar. Later she discarded punctuation except for numerous dashes; important words began with capitals. Her swift, breathless poems are bare of all but the essentials with the utmost condensation of thought. Deceptively simple, her poems are small, but her subjects are large. One is amazed at the abiding purity and profundity of her art.

Her earliest poem was embroidered on a sampler. It begins, "Jesus Permit Thy Gracious Name to Stand as the First Efforts of an Infant's Hand," and ends with the prayer that she may write His name upon her heart. Many of her late religious poems suggest that at the last, after all her doubts, His name *was* written on her heart.

"Emily Dickinson is one of the foremost masters of poetic English since Shakespeare, and in her severe economy of speech comparable to Dante" (Henry W. Wells).

Like all the greatest she stands alone.

Richard Sewall

BIBLIOGRAPHY

Bingham, Millicent Todd. *Ancestors' Brocades: The Literary Debut of Emily Dickinson.* New York: Harper and Brothers Publishers, 1945.

Poems reprinted from Dickinson, Emily. *Poems.* Boston: Roberts Brothers, 1891, 1895 and *Poems by Emily Dickinson.* Boston: Little, Brown, and Company, 1898.

Sewall, Richard B. *The Life of Emily Dickinson.* New York: Farrar, Straus, and Giroux, 1974.

Wells, Henry W. *Introduction to Emily Dickinson.* Chicago: Packard and Co., 1947.

Whicher, George F. *This Was a Poet: A Critical Biography of Emily Dickinson.* New York: Charles Scribner's and Sons, 1938.

RECOMMENDED READING

Dickinson, Emily. *Selected Poems of Emily Dickinson.* New York: Random House, The Modern Library, 1948.

GEORGE ELIOT

1819-1880

What do I think of Middlemarch?
What do I think of glory?

Emily Dickinson

In the Victorian age Great Britain reached the height of its power as an empire. The English people became high-minded, modest, self-righteous, enterprising, and very prim—sex was a taboo subject. This age produced a host of great novelists, such as Anthony Trollope and the Brontë sisters, but the greatest were Dickens, Thackery, and George Eliot.

What is extraordinary about George Eliot is that she achieved hardwon success in a male-dominated world. Some say she even thought like a man, but certainly she possessed one of the finest intellects of her time.

Mary Ann Evans (her real name) was born in 1819 (the same year as Queen Victoria). She was the daughter of a rural Warwickshire land agent by his second wife. Plain, clumsy, the little girl had a large head and showed no promise of beauty or of the great genius within her. However, her father was proud of her shining intelligence and called her "his little wench."

At the age of five she was sent to an evangelical boarding school and soon became an outstanding student with a profound thirst for knowledge. In her childhood loneliness she turned to books and developed a passion for reading that persisted throughout her life.

Eventually Mary Ann was able to read in various languages, including Homer in Greek. Above all else she loved the world of books—an interest essential to any creative literary artist. She developed an outstanding power to work creatively. She loved to roam the beautiful English countryside, storing up memories so important in her writing—a self-education that never ended.

As a child, she was extremely devout and read the Bible over and over again. Later her vigorous prose is based on a thorough familiarity with the King James Bible translation. During her school years, she was greatly influenced by her evangelical teacher, Maria Lewis, and other Bible-believing teachers and friends.

Unfortunately, she was a victim of night terrors that continued all her life. She often suffered poor health, depression, and later painful trouble with her teeth, but with courage and ambition she gave her best in everything she accomplished.

At the age of sixteen Mary Ann left school because of the death of her mother and soon took over the household duties—overseeing the dairy, baking, and preserve- and cheese-making. Her siblings had all left home, so for a long time she felt frustrated and alone in the world. Later she spoke of this period as "the long, sad years of youth."

Her father, Robert Evans, like many Victorians, was a man of strong evangelical Protestant convictions. He had had little schooling, but by his own efforts was successful in managing several large estates. He was hard-working and had a strong sense of duty and absolute integrity.

As a child, Mary Ann often rode about the estates with her father and learned the value of hard work, honesty, and the overcoming of difficulties. These lessons influenced her whole life. Her lifelong preference for the countryside was linked in her mind with her father's company. She was wholly tied to his habits. He was extremely demanding, so she sought to please him at whatever cost to herself.

After moving to Coventry with her father, she met the Brays, friendly neighbors who were free-thinking Unitarians. Through their liberal influence she gradually lost her evangelical faith, although she had been fervent in her beliefs until the age of twenty-seven. (The wrong kind of friends can be dangerous.) Reading Charles Hennell's *An Inquiry into the Origins of Christianity* confirmed her doubt, which she had been grappling with for years, and she became an agnostic.

Not wishing to be hypocritical, she refused to go to church with her father. Of course, her decision caused a violent rupture in their relationship. He would not speak to her for weeks, no longer understood her, and was unable to respond to her questioning mind. (She needed a place like L'Abri Fellowship where honest questions can be answered.)

Eventually there was a reconciliation, and for her father's last seven years, she attended church with him, although never returning to her evangelical roots. She both loved and resented her father, who was difficult and at times unkind. She nursed him through his last long illness, often reading his favorite Walter Scott novels out loud. An unmarried daughter shackled to the care of an aging parent was typical of that society's expectations for single women.

She took care of her father day and night, with little concern for her own needs, and so was utterly exhausted at his death. "What shall I be without my father?" she wrote. "It will seem as if part of my moral nature were gone." And yet had he lived another ten years, she probably would never have become a writer.

Victorian women were more subject to family pressures than the men. Robert Evans's great concern was that his daughter marry and certainly not that she earn a living. Her unloving brother Isaac also had enough thought of her welfare to urge her to get married.

She enjoyed reading the works of Jane Austen, who never married and remained financially dependent on her family most of her life. The arrangement gave Jane the freedom to write, and writing was possible for women because it could be done at home with materials easily available. A similar situation enabled the Brontës, Emily Dickinson, Beatrix Potter, and Christina Rossetti to develop their gifts.

During her father's illness in the early 1840s, Mary Ann became acquainted with higher German biblical criticism, introduced to her by her free-thinking friends. Over a period of two years she translated from German to English the voluminous *Life of Christ* by B. F. Strauss.

Strauss considered the gospel of mythical origin and dismissed all the miracles and supernatural elements. This secularization of religion was a powerful intellectual attack on biblical Christianity. It made Mary Ann ill to dissect the wonderful story of the Crucifixion. While translating, she worked with an image of Christ on the cross above her desk. Her turning from Christianity caused great conflict within herself and distress to her family and friends such as Maria Lewis. At times during this period, her life often seemed intolerable, for she knew her youth was passing away.

Mary Ann's remarkable genius was completely misunderstood by her family. Fortunately, she was able to escape their narrow-minded world after the death of her father. He left most of his estate to his other children, even bequeathing the set of Walter Scott novels to her sister Chrissey. But at last Mary Ann was free to make her own choices. To support herself she decided to become a writer. Something of an early feminist, she was brave, almost defiant, and possessed amazing determination.

Following her father's death in 1849, she fulfilled an old dream by spending several months in Geneva. Then she moved to London where she became the editor of the *Westminster Review*. However, like Charlotte Brontë, she remained a country girl at heart and felt ill when confined to a city.

She always needed a strong man to lean upon, needed to be loved. She had crushes on several men, including some who were married. Their minds attracted her. At one point she openly declared her love for the philosopher Herbert Spencer, but he rejected her. Lack of beauty was a detriment to her, and she was neither charming nor strongly feminine. Henry James said that this "great horse-faced genius was 'magnificently ugly, deliciously hideous.'" But she had a rich, lovely voice, a passionate nature, and intelligent eyes, and she was a superb conversationalist. She preferred men to women, although later in her life several women looked to her as their spiritual mother.

At the age of thirty-four, through Herbert Spencer she met the literary critic and writer George Lewes. He was a married man, unable to get a divorce from his wife although she was an adulteress with several illegitimate children. This was a time when free love was condoned among free thinkers. Mary Ann defied Victorian convention and lived with the man she loved, convinced that the circumstances preventing their marriage were unfair. She was liberated by her love for Lewes, finding fulfillment with him.

Lewes provided the conditions in which her genius could flourish, and through his urging she began to write her great novels. She took the pen name George Eliot—George because it was Lewes's name, and Eliot because it was a "good mouth-filling, easily pronounced word." For some years she was thought to be a male author.

Their mutual love endured and enriched the remainder of their twenty-five years together. They were superb helpmates. Her friends thought him a bit vulgar, but she didn't mind. She loved him and needed him to fulfill her potential. Lewes was not afraid of her mind—he gloried in it. Also a writer, he produced several books, including a fine biography of Goethe.

When George Eliot was thirty-five, she and Lewes went to Weimar, Germany, for several months, becoming friends with Franz Liszt and other notables. They always traveled as man and wife and were well received by friends and admirers. However, in Victorian England she was socially ostracized.

Writer Virginia Woolf thought that Mary Ann's happiness with Lewes released the spring of her creativity, and the social isolation threw her back upon herself and her memories. Her brother Isaac even caused all the family to break completely with her. Only after the death of Lewes, when two years later she married John Cross, did she hear from Isaac. By then she was very famous and quite wealthy.

In spite of poor health the Leweses were rugged travelers about England and the Continent, especially drawn to the warmth of Italy. They were always observing, working on projects, and in the evenings reading a great deal out loud together.

George Eliot was a tireless writer of letters, which reminds one that a literary career often begins with letter-writing or keeping a diary. Lewes acted successfully as the agent for her fiction. With his three sons to educate, they had to live frugally, but after her early triumph in the writing of books, she was earning large sums of money.

"Polly" (as Lewes enjoyed calling her) had been on the verge of middle age when at thirty-seven she wrote her first fiction, *Scenes of Clerical Life*. The work included three novellas with most of the characters and settings taken from real life, which caused a furor in Warwickshire. However, the literary reviews were good and gave her courage to continue writing. Her excellent publisher was John Blackwood.

In 1859 *Adam Bede*, dedicated to Lewes, appeared and was an immediate and lasting success with the public. She remarked that this pastoral novel would be "full of the breath of cows and the scent of hay," and it was. In the character of Adam Bede she celebrated all that was admirable in her father. The book contrasts Hetty Sorel, a pretty, flirtatious, simpleminded girl, with Dinah Morris, an earnest, devout evangelical preacher. Adam longs to marry Hetty, but she is seduced by a rich, young squire. She murders the baby born of that liaison and is sent away from England. Later Adam marries Dinah.

Another character in the book is Mrs. Poyser, the gem of the story with her shrewd sense of humor (humor is rare in George Eliot's works when compared to Shakespeare and Dickens). Among many amusing comments, Mrs. Poyser says, "It's but little good you'll do watering last year's crops," and "He was like a cock who thought the sun had risen to hear him crow."

Adam Bede abounds in tributes to Christian virtue. One of Eliot's favorite characters was the preacher Dinah Morris. Here are several quotes relating to Dinah. ". . . as if, even when she was speaking, her soul was in prayer reposing on an unseen support." In one of her sermons Dinah says, "Ah! dear friends, we are in sad want of good news about God; and what does other good news signify if we haven't that? For everything else comes to an end, and when we die, we leave it all. But God lasts when everything else is gone. What shall we do if He is not our friend?" "No wonder man's religion has much sorrow in it; no wonder he needs a suffering God." "Whether we live or die, we are in the presence of God."

The Mill on the Floss was published in 1860 when Mary Ann and Lewes were in Rome. They made a practice of being out of the country when her books were published. The book is basically autobiographical, with Maggie the young Mary Ann, Isaac as Tom, Chrissey as Lucy, and the Dobson sisters, Eliot's much disliked aunts, as the Pearsons. Even the countryside resembles that around her childhood home at Griff. The heavy plot is like her own life. The dominating passion of her youth was for her brother Isaac, called Tom in this novel, who rejected her. At the dramatic ending Tom and Maggie drown together in the River Floss.

In 1861 one of George Eliot's most admired works, *Silas Marner*, appeared and met with enthusiastic acclaim. This poetic novel is a true masterpiece. It concerns a lonely weaver whose miserly life is transformed when he decides to raise an "orphan" who wanders into his house. As in her other writings, Eliot emphasizes morality, duty, and love.

Her next book, *Romola*, was a long, ponderous historical novel that met with neither financial nor critical success. *Saturday Review* expressed the general opinion: "No reader of *Romola* will lay it down without admiration, and few with regret." The story takes place in Florence during the rule of Savonarola, 1452-1498, when the Medici had been forced out of the city. The deep moral tone is impressive, although the book seems unnecessarily wordy and overblown with far too much detail. Years later Willa Cather countered these over-full novels with her *demeublé* books (that is, books such as *The Lost Lady*, without extra "furniture").

After *Felix Holt* her greatest work, *Middlemarch*, appeared in 1871-72, and it was immediately recognized as a masterpiece. The novel presents a panoramic view of nineteenth-century English provincial life, recreating a whole society. Eliot deals with the problem of a gifted young woman, Dorothea, who longs to do something worthwhile in life at a time when marrying or becoming a governess were the only options.

Dorothea marries a dusty, aged clergyman, Casaubon, and the marriage is a failure. Eliot's heroines cannot live without religion, but they no longer know to whom to pray. The other main character, Dr. Lydgate, marries a silly, wasteful girl and runs into debt. The banker, Bulstrode, a religious hypocrite, is also ruined financially.

Caleb Garth, like Adam Bede, is George Eliot's father, and Caleb's daughter Mary is delightful. *Middlemarch* is a remarkable, penetrating psychological work. Emily Dickinson once said, "What do I think of *Middlemarch*? What do I think of glory?"

George Eliot insisted she could never have written her novels, especially *Middlemarch*, without the help of Lewes. He sheltered her from harsh criticism and constantly encouraged her, as she was often full of doubt, sensitive to criticism, and in poor health. Her last novel was *Daniel Deronda*.

She was greatly praised for her writing but shrank from fame. When living with Lewes at The Priory, people such as the Russian novelist Turgenev, Anthony Trollope, Robert Browning, and several women who thought of her as their spiritual mother flocked to her on Sunday afternoons. Dickens's amusing comment was, "On Sunday I hope to attend service at The Priory!" Her fame was awesome.

Eliot had an astonishing intellectual vitality. She read widely in various languages, including Greek and Hebrew, and was a fine pianist. Her poetry does not have a singing quality, with the exception of the lines:

> *O may I join the Choir invisible*
> *Of those immortal dead who live again*
> *In minds made better by their presence.*

She was acquainted with many nonbelieving intellectuals and kept up with current events, but she never returned to her childhood faith. She was a strong-minded woman and became very touchy and rather pompous in her later years. She sought to replace Christianity with the "religion of humanity." The doctrine of sympathy was her substitute for the faith she had lost. She had read the German philosopher Feuerbach, who believed that in the absence of God, the dominating motive of human relationships must be love.

After Lewes's sudden death from cancer in 1878, Eliot went into deep mourning and wrote no more. In spite of never being able to marry Lewes, her fame and honor caused the circumstances of her private life to be overlooked. Two years later she married John Cross, twenty years her junior, whom she had known for years. She had a lifelong need of a strong man to lean on. She said, "I am quite flourishing again in my rickety fashion, a mended piece of antique furniture."

While they honeymooned in Venice, John Cross tried to commit suicide by jumping from the hotel into the Grand Canal, but he was pulled out by gondoliers. Nevertheless, Mary Ann was very happy with him, especially because her brother Isaac broke the silence of twenty-three years with a letter congratulating her on her marriage. Unfortunately she died suddenly of kidney failure at sixty-one, only seven months after the wedding. John Cross wrote her first biography.

At the end of her life she was regarded as a great moral teacher, a deep thinker, and a remarkable psychologist. Her novels are penetratingly philosophical. Not really a feminist, she was at heart deeply conservative. The Bible was lying by her bed when she died, as well as *The Imitation of Christ*.

Her enthusiasm for the evangelical movement, to which she was introduced by the school mistress Marie Lewis, revealed a deeply religious temperament that was to dictate her actions throughout her life, even after she rejected orthodox Christianity. She thought that evangelicalism crushed creativity, which is untrue when we think of Bach, Handel, Milton, Dürer, Rembrandt, Bunyan, Jane Austen, Christina Rossetti, the Brontës, and so on.

She went through agonizing struggles with many obstacles—her gender; bad health with endless headaches, eye strain, and fatigue; a plain appearance; the conventions of her day—but as an overcomer she triumphed and made a brilliant success of her career.

BIBLIOGRAPHY

Haight, G. S. *George Eliot: A Biography*. London: Penguin Books, 1992.

Laski, Margharita. *George Eliot*. New York: Thames and Hudson, 1973.

RECOMMENDED READING

Scenes of Clerical Life
Adam Bede
The Mill on the Floss
Silas Marner: The Weaver of Raveloe
Romola
Middlemarch

FLANNERY O'CONNOR

1925-1964

*I see from the standpoint of Christian orthodoxy. This means that for
me the meaning of life is centered in our redemption by Christ,
and what I see in the world I see in its relation to that.*

Flannery O'Connor

*Flannery O'Connor was "tough minded, laconic, with a marvelous
wit and an absolute absence of self-pity. She made me understand,
as never before or since, what spiritual heroism and beauty can be."*

Richard Gilman

Mary Flannery O'Connor was born on March 25, 1925, in Savannah, Georgia, into a family with a Roman Catholic heritage. Her parents were Edward and Regina Cline O'Connor. In 1938 the family moved to Milledgeville, Georgia, which had been the state capitol before the Civil War.

At an early age Flannery became fascinated with all manner of fowls—chickens, ducks, geese, pheasants, peacocks, and swans. In her amusing story, "The King of the Birds," she tells of an experience that marked her for life. She had a chicken who was able to walk backwards as easily as forwards. *Pathé News* sent a photographer from New York to capture this unusual bird on film. Young Flannery concluded, "Since that big event, my life has been an anticlimax."

In high school in a home economics course, she was asked to make a garment suitable for a small child. O'Connor arrived in class not with a child but with a chicken in tow. The bird was neatly attired in a white piqué coat and a stylishly belted back.

The early death of her father from lupus in 1941 and her own later illness with the same disease probably influenced the concern in her writing with omnipresent death and disaster. This awareness of death as an inescapable fact of existence charges her work with a powerful tension and places her in the line of great tragic writers such as Dostoevsky. She was also preoccupied with belief in grace and the devil.

After graduating from Georgia State College for Women in 1945, she attended a writer's workshop at the University of Iowa. When she was interviewed for the course by Paul Engle, he was quite unable to understand her Southern accent, so he asked her to write out her name and background. Soon Engle knew he had an "original" who knew her own mind and possessed a fierce devotion to good writing.

Her principal vocation, as a Catholic and a Southerner, was to write stories. She felt that the Southern writer has the advantage of a "storytelling habit," and being from the Bible Belt, as H. L. Mencken called it, has a knowledge of the Bible and a sense of history. She said, "Southern writers are stuck with the South, and it's a very good thing to be stuck with."

Her first short story, "The Geranium," was published the summer of 1946 in *Accent*. Other stories followed, making their way into various prestigious journals. For years very little money came in. She said ironically, "If you want to write well and live well at the same time, you better arrange to inherit money."

In 1948 she resided briefly in Yaddo, New York, a writers' haven, where she became a friend of the poet Robert Lowell. Here she began work on her novel *Wise Blood*, which took five years to complete. She wrote slowly, diligently, and prayerfully and called herself a traditional writer. She was constantly revising, improving, or throwing away what was unsatisfactory, for she had the "habit of perfectionism." As a writer Flannery dropped her first name Mary, because as she said, "Who was likely to buy the stories of an Irish washer woman?"

In 1949 O'Connor lived with Sally and Robert Fitzgerald in Connecticut. Because of their literary work, they became close friends with her for the rest of her short life. They edited her book of lectures and essays, *Mystery and Manners*, and the collection of her letters, *The Habit of Being*.

Letters were always important to her, and she was a prolific correspondent. Her close friendships were sustained through correspondence, and she was generous in answering inquiries from students. *The Habit of Being* is so communicative that it reads like a novel. Asked about a crank letter she received, she responded, "Some old lady said that my book left a bad taste in her mouth. I wrote back to her and said, 'You weren't supposed to eat it.'"

In December 1950 Flannery had her first major attack of lupus, a terrifying and painful disease related to arthritis. There was no cure. She had only been fifteen when her father died of the disease. After that first attack, Flannery was no longer able to walk upstairs and eventually had to use aluminum crutches. She and her mother, Regina, moved to a dairy farm called Andalusia outside of Milledgeville.

Regina ran the farm with high efficiency. Flannery was amusingly devoted to her demanding mother and often referred to her as "parent." Regina appears in several of Flannery's short stories. When asked if she was able to work on the farm, Flannery quickly responded, "No, I'm a writer. Don't make me out a farm girl. All I know about the land is it's underneath me." Again deadly serious but relentlessly comic, she observed about lupus: "The disease is no consequence to my writing since for that I use my head and not my feet." Note the saving grace of humor.

Flannery wrote every morning, even Sunday, for three hours and then spent the rest of the day recuperating, largely in the society of ducks. "If I waited for inspiration, I'd still be waiting."

Some days she would sit at the typewriter in her downstairs room, and all that was typed ended in the wastepaper basket. Even so, she enjoyed writing and saved her diminished strength just for that. In a letter to Robert Lowell she mused, "I have enough energy to write with, and as that is all I have any business doing anyhow, I can with one eye squinted take it all as a blessing."

Nathaniel Hawthorne and Joseph Conrad were among her favorite writers; she is indebted stylistically to Mark Twain. She called herself "a very innocent speller" and enjoyed writing words as they sounded with a Southern accent, such as *bisnis* or *bidniss*. One of America's most original and provocative authors, she was able to blend the comic and the serious with a sensitive imagination into salty comedy. She said, "Mine is a comic art, but that does not detract from its seriousness."

Her style is remarkably transparent and her dialogue superb. The beauty of her language sometimes suggests a King James version of the Southern dialect, as she used the Old Testament for her background. A very honest writer, she is never dull but often shocking. Her range is narrow and themes repetitious. Yet within her limits she has a fine control of dialogue and symbol. "A great master of the short story, she wrote thirty-three stories and two brief novels that have a perfection of art and form that few other writers have" (Mary Mumbach).

O'Connor attended mass every day when able and was unshakable in her Roman Catholic orthodoxy. She produced fiction filled with Christian images and that at the same time was grotesque and violent. She writes about man cut off from God's grace by a tawdry world and yet yearning for God and finding Him through terrible torments. She writes about an abnormal world of fools, charlatans, killers, and lunatics—in some ways reminiscent of Poe. One critic has considered her fiction a twentieth century version, in words, of a medieval cathedral. It is populated with gargoyles and peculiar halved saints.

Yet her characters are always liable to be saved by God's inexplicable mercy. "My subject in fiction is the action of grace in territory held largely by the devil." "We lost our innocence in the Fall, and our return to it is through the redemption which was brought about by Christ's death" (*Mystery and Manners*). She believed that the acceptance of grace brought freedom in a fallen world.

In the 1950s Flannery discerned an imperturbable smugness, flatulent optimism, and crass self-righteousness in society around her that she had to expose. She used the harshest means of attack with brilliantly created characterizations. She commented, "When you are speaking [writing], you have to speak loudly so they will understand." A woman in *Wise Blood* is said to be "so well adjusted she no longer had to think." In "The Displaced Person" Mrs. Shortley "felt that religion was essentially for those people who didn't have the brains to avoid evil without it." Flannery believed that all people are displaced persons in need of divine grace.

O'Connor observed that her stories are hard because there is nothing harder or less sentimental than Christian realism. In order to show light she had to show darkness. Devout but not pietistic, she enjoyed the folly-ridden world of the absurd. Here is a quote from her short story "Greenleaf:" "Mrs. May winced. She thought the word, 'Jesus' should be kept inside the church building like other words inside the bedroom. She was a good Christian woman with a large respect for religion, though she did not, of course, believe any of it was true."

O'Connor's first novel, *Wise Blood*, was published in 1952. It has become a classic of twentieth-century literature. Her comment on writing a novel: "Well, I just kind of feel it out like a hound dog. I follow the scent." She also remarked that writing a novel is a terrible experience during which the hair often falls out and the teeth decay. Loneliness was also a part of that experience, but she knew that writers thrive on isolation.

In *Wise Blood* O'Connor describes the ugliness, crudity, and shallowness of much pseudo-Christianity and the "church without Christ." She believed the South is hardly Christ-centered but is Christ-haunted. In her note to the second edition, she writes, "It is a comic novel about a Christian *malgré lui*, and as such, very serious, for all comic novels that are any good must be about a matter of life and death."

Wise Blood is the story of Hazel Motes, a twenty-two-year-old sinner-saint caught in the struggle against his innate desperate faith. A runaway from God, his conflict is between rationalism and his "God-sense." He founds the Church of Christ without Christ and uses a broken-down car as his pulpit, which is destroyed by the police. Finally his God-haunted soul sins "well" because his actions lead to redemption. Before his death Motes blinds himself so he can really see.

Flannery began to receive national attention and was asked her opinion on contemporary literature. "I hate to deliver opinions. On most things I don't deserve an opinion, and on a lot of things I simply don't have an opinion."

By no means a "popular writer," but a profound one, she remarked with dry humor, "Everywhere I go, I'm asked if I think the universities stifle writers. My opinion is that they don't stifle enough of them. There's many a bestseller that could have been prevented by a good teacher . . . if these people can learn to write badly enough, they can make a great deal of money."

She could be cutting about writers she thought were frauds. She had strong opinions and did not hesitate to express them, especially in her letters. "In the South there are more amateur authors than there are rivers and streams." However, Flannery believed that the best writing in her time was being done in the South, which critics referred to as the Southern Literary Renaissance. The reason, she thought, was that the region is the Bible Belt, and it is the Bible that defines absolutes and the mystery of the supernatural.

She commented further: "The fact that Catholics don't see religion through the Bible is a deficiency in Catholics. The Catholic novelist can learn a great deal from the Protestant South. The Bible is what we share with all Christians, and the Old Testament we share with all Jews."

"There are qualities that make fiction. One is the sense of mystery, and the other is the sense of manners. . . . To ensure our sense of mystery we need a sense of evil which sees the devil as a real spirit. . . . As a Southern writer one doesn't have to go anywhere for manners, bad or good; we've got them in abundance" (*Mystery and Manners*).

"I have heard it said," O'Connor wrote, "that belief in Christian dogma is a hindrance to the writer, but I myself have found nothing further from the truth. Actually, it frees the storyteller to observe. The Christian lives in a larger universe, as the natural world contains the supernatural. My own feeling is that writers who see by the light of their Christian faith have the sharper eyes for the grotesque, for the perverse, and for the unacceptable. The Christian novelist is distinguished from his pagan colleagues by recognizing sin as sin."

Although on crutches and limited in energy, Flannery was not sedentary and was able to travel alone to various universities, such as Hollins (Jane Stuart Smith's alma mater) to give lectures. She received many honorary awards during her lifetime. Not prone to indulge in idle chatter, she found interviews tiresome. After one she wrote to her friend Cecil Dawkins, "I always feel like a dry cow being milked. There is no telling what they will get out of you. . . . If you do manage to say anything that makes sense, they put down the opposite."

One of the great pleasures of Flannery's life was books. She read widely and deeply, especially theological literature. With her quick wit she commented, "You have to realize the genuine stupidity of the reader . . . his average mental age is thirteen years." She felt the lack of a large intelligent audience that believes Christ is God. "It takes readers as well as writers to make literature."

Her own favorite short story was "The Artificial Nigger," in which she suggested the redemptive quality of the suffering of African-Americans. She believed that the uneducated Southern Black was not the clown he was made out to be. He was a man of very elaborate manners and great formality, which he used superbly for his own protection and to insure his own privacy. She believed that the Bible gives meaning and dignity to the lives of the poor people of the South.

A slow, complex, thorny writer, Flannery O'Connor produced about two stories a year. She sought to make the natural world real in order to stress the supernatural and often wrote about the cruel, sardonic, terrifying world of the abnormal. She could be impatient, opinionated, doubtful, modest, delighted by compliments, and distressed at unfavorable reviews. Although she had a rather shy manner, there was no foolishness about her, and she had tremendous inner strength. She was at first misunderstood by the Christian community, but she knew she was a good writer.

Her second novel, *The Violent Bear It Away*, was published in 1960. The writing took her seven years, and the book is considered her masterpiece. Old Tarwater, the backwoods prophet, is the hero of the novel, and O'Connor said that she was 100 percent behind him. Christ was the center of Old Tarwater's life.

Old Tarwater's great nephew, young Tarwater, is the central character, a sinner-saint like Hazel Motes of *Wise Blood*. Both men struggle against the world, the flesh, and the devil.

Section I. Young Tarwater travels from the country to the city. O'Connor uses the city inhabitants to give a sense of the hollow, mechanized, and rationally reduced life of modern man. The people in the city through positive thinking (nonintellectuals) and positivism (intellectuals) hide from the eye of God. The sun is a symbol of God's eye and is dulled in the city. Burning is a unifying factor in this many-layered novel, as Tarwater sets fire to the house and later the grove.

Section II. Tarwater lives with his Uncle Rayber, a rationalistic schoolteacher. Rayber tries to persuade Tarwater to give up Christianity, but Tarwater is deeply disturbed and runs away.

Section III. Tarwater becomes a stranger to man's city and returns to God's violent country (Matt. 11:12). Finally he journeys back to the city as a prophet-bearer of God's Word. He sets his face toward the dark city where the children of God are sleeping.

O'Connor's poetic prose is vivid: ". . . as they sped forward on the black untwisting highway watched on either side by a dark wall of trees." She described eyes in a variety of ways. The O. T. and E. T. twins had "bright grasping fox-colored eyes like their father" ("Greenleaf"). "His eyes were like two bright nails behind his gold-rimmed spectacles" ("The Displaced Person").

Flannery's favorite bird, the peacock, is a traditional symbol of Christ's divinity and the Resurrection. Her faith in Christian doctrine furnished her with a sense of historical continuity from Christ's time on earth to her own day. She believed that the Resurrection of Christ is the high point of nature and that redemption through Him is meaningless to us unless we recognize our need for it.

"I see God as all-perfect, all-complete, all-powerful. God is love. I believe man is created in God's image. It makes a difference in a novel whether the writer believes we are created in God's image or whether we create God in our own," wrote O'Connor.

One may disagree with some of Flannery's theological beliefs, but at the center of her work is a true Christian sense of existence. For her, belief in Christ is a matter of life and death, but to many it is a matter of no great consequence. Either we are serious about salvation, or we are not.

"The Christian will feel that whatever his initial gift is, it comes from God." O'Connor wrote the best she could for the sake of returning her talent, increased, to the invisible God to use or not to use as He saw fit.

One of O'Connor's last short stories, "Revelation," is among her finest. After many times in the hospital, she died at age thirty-nine at the height of her powers and left us marvels in her work. Her reputation is now worldwide, but her roots are in Georgia. She is not just a Southern writer but, like William Faulkner, a universal writer. "Her talent for fiction is so great as to be overwhelming" (Orville Prescott in the *New York Times*).

BIBLIOGRAPHY

Coles, Robert. *Flannery O'Connor's South.* Baton Rouge: Louisiana State University Press, 1980.

Magee, Rosemary M., ed. *Conversations with Flannery O'Connor.* Jackson: University Press of Mississippi, 1987.

Walters, Dorothy. *Flannery O'Connor.* Boston: Twayne Publishers, 1973.

RECOMMENDED READING

Complete Short Stories
Wise Blood
The Violent Bear It Away
Mystery and Manners
The Habit of Being

BEATRIX POTTER

1866-1943

*Her mind was exceptionally alert, and she was rarely
bored, for she had the invaluable gift of being able to amuse
herself with her own thoughts; she also exercised her brain by
such self-imposed tasks as learning many of the plays of
Shakespeare until she was word-perfect.*

Maggie Lane

Margaret Lane said in her fine book, *The Magic Years of Beatrix Potter,* "Her little books had been the joy of my childhood." Indeed, Beatrix Potter's books are pure magic, and she is one of the most celebrated creators of children's books who ever lived. Her works show great originality and are of timeless value. Simple and direct, with never an extra word, they depict the exquisite beauty of the English countryside.

Potter's talking-beast tales, over twenty in number, were produced in about thirteen years—an amazing achievement. However, this creativity was preceded by a great deal of hard work, accompanied by loneliness and depression. One wonders if loneliness is one of the requirements for creativity.

Helen Beatrix Potter was born in London at Bolton Gardens ("my unbeloved birthplace"). Her world had little appreciation for childhood, although this was the generation introduced to *Alice in Wonderland*. Beatrix was even dressed like Alice in light, uncomfortable clothes. She lived at Bolton Gardens, unwillingly for the most part, for the next forty-seven years, more or less a captive or slave to her parents. She was rarely allowed to go out.

Her parents, Rupert and Helen, had inherited money from *trade* (a word they both disliked), so they had an exceedingly comfortable lifestyle on their unearned income. Rupert was able to retire early from practicing law, and they became members of the idle rich. They were snobbish and disagreeable, with a strict routine in their lives that often suffocated Beatrix. Mrs. Potter lived largely for her needlework. She was disapproving, remote, implacable, and had no interest in her daughter's artistry.

The parents assumed that Beatrix was content to live with them and to take care of them in their old age. She was their appendage. They were Unitarians, so they did not even have the joy of celebrating Christmas in their home, and there was no family affection to take its place. Beatrix was dutiful but inwardly felt resentment and frustration.

However, her father took her often to museums and art exhibits. What drew father and daughter together was photography, from which Beatrix learned to love nature and observe it carefully. She also learned to paint pictures.

Her father's contemporary as a photographer was author Lewis Carroll, who also photographed many well-known people, including the Pre-Raphaelite Rossetti family. Rupert often worked with the painter Millais, so Beatrix was introduced to one of the famous art studios of her day. Best of all, she spent long, quiet afternoons in the Natural History Museum sketching insects, mushrooms, stuffed animals, and so on. She became a true and serious naturalist.

She was entirely self-taught in her art, except for drawing lessons. She was never allowed to go to school, for in those days only boys went to school, or to have friends, because her parents believed she might catch diseases from them. She had governesses who taught her at home.

After her younger brother Bertram went away to school, she was very lonely and became exceedingly shy. Although she often suffered from depression, headaches, tiredness, and insomnia, she was not unhappy, having a cheerful disposition. And yet she said at nineteen, "I am terribly afraid of the future," and often felt her life was wasted.

She liked the solitude of her third-story room where she kept a miniature zoo of mice, rabbits, hedgehogs, frogs, and so forth. These animals that she loved were her real friends and became like people to her. She was not afraid of the dark, nor was she bored. She led a hermit-like, reclusive existence, and in her loneliness created a world of her own.

From early years she was constantly drawing and benefited from lessons from age twelve to seventeen. She had a passion to sketch and do water coloring. "I must draw, however poor the result." She kept her vast numbers of drawings in a large chest. To Beatrix the boredom of doing nothing was intolerable. From early childhood she had a creative urge, but it was years later before she found the key that opened the way for her to produce her exquisite "little books."

Alone with her animals, she had a thirst for her work that was like a fever—drawing, painting, writing in her diary. This neatly written little book was in a secret code in a small hand, as though inscribed by a mouse. She started the diary at age fifteen and kept it up until age thirty (more than 200,000 words). Only recently has it been deciphered, and it provides interesting details about her artistic growth.

She had a tenacious memory from early childhood and noticed everything, especially in nature. Later, to occupy empty hours, she memorized many of Shakespeare's plays and would recite them to herself letter perfect when unable to sleep.

Of the extended Easter and summer vacations with her parents, she wrote, "It is somewhat trying to pass a season of enjoyment in the company of persons who are constantly on the outlook for matters of complaint." "Our summer 'holiday' is always a weary business."

Yet the three months in Scotland and the north country (for over twelve years) was an escape from dreary city life. She had an opportunity to observe and make beautiful sketches of the nature she loved. In these difficult days she was gathering material for her great life work. In her youth she said, "I wish I was not always short of money." She could not imagine what her royalties would eventually bring to her.

She at first made scientific drawings of mushrooms, but as her parents did not approve of these, she began to study nursery rhyme pictures by Randolph Caldecott, especially rabbits. She worked for years searching for some way to bring her art to fruition.

At age twenty-four she sold some of her illustrated Christmas cards—the beginning of her publishing career. She had spent her youth painting and drawing. That had become a consuming passion. Now she must find an outlet.

A favorite governess, Annie Moore, had eight children, and Beatrix loved this family. Sometimes she was allowed to visit them, but between visits she sent the children picture letters. Fortunately, the youngsters prized these letters and kept them.

When one of the children, five-year-old Noel, was ill, she wrote him a story about her pet bunny called Peter. She had no idea that in writing these picture letters, at last she had found the magic key.

Seven years later, in her mid-thirties, she decided on a new venture, a modest children's book (there were many being written at this time). She borrowed back her letter from Noel. Her interest was to paint animal scenes to please herself and other people's children. She diligently sent off this little manuscript (which she had turned into a story) with black-and-white drawings to six different publishers. The manuscript was relentlessly refused, often returned without thanks.

Very persistent and not expecting anything to come easily, she decided to publish it herself with personal savings. She had 450 copies printed. Obliging aunts and friends bought them. She had the courage to send the little book again to Warne Publishers. They agreed to publish it if she did colored illustrations. It was an immediate and ongoing success.

Peter Rabbit (1901) was a milestone in children's literature and marked the beginning of the modern picture book. There is a perfect union between the text and the beautifully composed water colors. The animals are dressed up like human country folks pursuing their activities in fresh English lanes and meadows or in cozy interiors beautifully rendered. Two of the greatest talking-beast masterpieces are *Peter Rabbit* and *Wind in the Willows*. But there are many more.

As Beatrix finished redoing the drawings of *Peter Rabbit*, she was already sketching for *The Tailor of Gloucester*. The book was written as a Christmas present for a young girl. Thinking it was too soon to send this story to her publisher, she paid to have 500 copies printed. It remained her own favorite among her works.

She loved nursery rhymes. Some are in *The Tailor*. Also included in this book is the old legend that all beasts can talk on the night between Christmas Eve and Christmas Day. She called *The Tailor* her "mouse book" because of the major part mice play in the story. One of her many tame mice, Hunca Munca, played an important role in another exquisite book, *The Tale of Two Bad Mice*.

She wrote and dedicated her books to children and tried them out in letter form on the various children of whom she was especially fond. (It is important to have an audience for whom to write.) Although she was rather timid in the presence of children, she said, "I made stories to please myself because I never grew up." She also said, "My usual way of writing is to scribble, and cut out, and write it again and again. The shorter and plainer the better. And read the Bible (unrevised version . . .) if I feel my style wants chastening."

She attended no church but knew the Bible well, and in her down days she was comforted by reading Scripture.

In spite of her timidity, she had a warm relationship with her publishers, the Warnes, and their lively family. She was intensely interested in the business of publishing. At the age of forty she became engaged to Norman Warne, who had been so helpful in giving her advice about her books.

Her parents were very upset that she had agreed to marry a man "in trade." Only a few weeks later he died of pernicious anemia. Deeply grieved, Beatrix received no sympathy from her parents. For consolation she returned to writing children's books for another five years. She usually did two books annually in these amazingly creative thirteen years.

Because of her love of the land and farming, she bought Hill Top Farm in Sawrey with her increasing royalties. Eventually she owned half of the village. Sawrey, in the lake district, is lovingly depicted in her books, especially *Hill Top Farm*. *The Tale of Jemima Puddle-duck* includes enchanting water colors of Hill Top Farm.

Her parents refused to let her live at the farm, but in her travels back and forth she carried along a pet rabbit (Peter and/or Benjamin Bunny), the hedgehog Mrs. Tiggy-Winkle, or a pet frog that she had for over five years. This pet frog, who accompanied her on extensive journeys, reminds us of her wonderful story *The Tale of Mr. Jeremy Fisher*.

Her fame and royalties increased, but she was still the captive of her Victorian parents. However, she continued to buy property in Sawrey through her lawyer, William Heelis, who was several years her junior. At age forty-seven, she finally escaped into marriage and became Mrs. William Heelis. Fame meant little to her, but she valued the comfort of having money. Happily married, she left off creativity to fulfill her interest in farming. Her creative life was over (partly because of failing eyesight and partly due to the work of the farm). "When I had no more to say, I had the sense to stop!" she explained.

Outspoken and opinionated (she was opposed to the women's vote), she could be rude, possibly because of her fame. But the shepherds and farm folk admired her. After her death, her ashes were scattered over a field above Sawrey. You can find this field in *The Tale of Jemima Puddle-duck*.

A few remaining thoughts: Beatrix illustrated only her own stories. She enjoyed inventing tales, but drawing was very difficult for her. Her stories had a beginning, an exciting middle section, and like fairy tales a good ending. From babyhood Beatrix had a passion for the paint box and pencil so that her desk drawers were full of drawings and illustrated letters. They were a gold mine of source material. "I do so hate finishing books; I would like to go on with them for years." Again she said, "It takes years for an idea to take shape"—for example, *The Fairy Caravan*.

She had a preference for inexpensive books—"all my little friends happen to be shilling people." She thought a children's book should have only one or two simple sentences and a picture on each page. Indeed, young children even before they read can quickly understand the story through the pictures. Introducing children to her books helps to open their eyes at an early age to some of the world's most delightful art.

Her books bring together grownups and children in a shared delight. Her unique genius and modesty, along with her ironic sense of humor and the dewy freshness of her landscapes, stir our imaginations. Although she never left the British Isles, her books have traveled the world in many languages. She wrote in a letter, "I think I have little friends all over the world." We need to introduce small children to Beatrix Potter—for their good and ours.

BIBLIOGRAPHY

Lane, Margaret. *The Magic Years of Beatrix Potter*. London: Warne and Co., 1978.

_____. *The Tale of Beatrix Potter: A Biography*. London: Warne and Co., 1971.

RECOMMENDED READING

All of Potter's books are worth reading, especially:

The Tale of Peter Rabbit

The Tale of Squirrel Nutkin

The Tailor of Gloucester

The Tale of Two Bad Mice

The Tale of Mrs. Tiggy-Winkle

The Tale of Mr. Jeremy Fisher

The Tale of Jemima Puddle-duck

CHRISTINA ROSSETTI

1830-1894

*For he who much has suffered,
much will know.*

Homer

L ong before Christina Rossetti was twenty, she was writing verses about all that she found most beautiful in nature and in her imagination. Yet another part of her brilliant mind was chanting, *"vanitas, vantitatum"* (vanity, all is vanity). That might sound like a contradiction, but she saw life from a Christian perspective. She recognized the beauty, wonder, and variety that coexist in the world with suffering, hardships, and a multitude of unexplained difficulties.

Even though Christina lived much of her life with little money, poor health, and unattained goals (she was engaged twice but never married, because of religious differences), she developed an amazing serenity and cheerfulness. Particularly later in life, she exhibited considerable down-to-earth common sense and humor. This serenity can only be explained by her Christian faith, which brought her joy even in a succession of serious illnesses.

While these trials inclined her to melancholy, they did not hinder her creative thinking nor interrupt her writing. Beneath the humble, quiet, and saintly life that others saw, lay a passionate Italian temperament. She had an Italian ear for harmony, and she delighted in beauty.

Born in London, Christina, her older sister Maria, and two brothers, William and Dante Gabriel, were educated at home by their mother, who had been a governess before her marriage. Frances Rossetti had a strong faith in God. She read to her children from the Bible, St. Augustine, and *Pilgrim's Progress*. She taught them the catechism and introduced them to many other books that broadened their outlook. *The Arabian Nights* was one of Christina's favorites.

A highly cultured woman of English and Italian background, Frances had an interest in writing poetry. She would often say, "If we cannot do all that we would like, let us do all that we can." Frances was deeply loved and respected by her children, and she was the delight of Christina's heart. Many of Christina's poems were dedicated to her.

Christina had a sunny childhood, although she was accused of being snappish and had a reputation for willfulness and temper. Once her mother said whimsically, "I have never received a valentine from anyone." Each year afterwards Christina not only gave her mother a valentine but also included an original poem. Christina was rarely separated from her mother for fifty-five years.

Christina's father, Gabriele, was also a poet. A political refugee from near Naples, Italy, he became a professor of Italian at King's College, Oxford. He was a Dante scholar and could quote the entire *Divine Comedy* from memory. The family was bilingual. Frances spoke English, and Gabriele always spoke in Italian.

This remarkable family lived in various dingy homes in the Bloomsbury area of London, surrounded by Italian exiles and English artists. In this exciting atmosphere, the parents and children often spent their evenings in front of the parlor fireplace, generally with a friendly cat lying by the warm fire. Literature, especially the Italian classics, and painting were enthusiastically discussed. Consequently, Christina, her sister, and two brothers all became writers. It certainly reminds one of the Brontë family.

Christina's brother Dante Gabriel, whose work is highly original, was one of the most famous English poets and painters of the 1800s. This family made a deep impression on English art and literature.

In 1847, when Christina was seventeen, her grandfather, Polidori, published some of her first poems. They already prefigured the richness of her vision and marked her formal literary debut. Not surprisingly, Christina always felt much affection for her grandfather and loved visiting his country home.

> *One day in the country*
> *Is worth a month in town.*

In her teens Christina suffered a nervous breakdown. Depression and a sense of guilt troubled her often, yet melancholy was the wellspring of her writing. Adolescent breakdown wasn't uncommon among Victorian girls as they sought to fit the mold of sweetness, submission, and self-sacrifice. Elizabeth Barrett at fifteen developed a disabling illness that turned her into an invalid. Catherine Booth became an invalid before finding her vocation as cofounder of the Salvation Army. Because of her inability to satisfy her desire for meaningful work, Florence Nightingale suffered recurrent collapses and then eventually founded the nursing profession as we know it today. Soldiers in the Crimean War called her the "Lady with the Lamp," a title both literal and figurative. Christina's Aunt Polidori at one time had worked with Florence Nightingale.

To recuperate from her breakdown, Christina was sent to the seaside. Though it was a lonely place, she greatly enjoyed walking along the shore searching for colored stones. She took along to the beach a load of books. For the remainder of her life she loved the restorative power of the seashore. Another diversion to lift her spirits was the zoo, to which she always took a goodly bag of eatables for the various animals.

Her brother Dante Gabriel, always Christina's warmest admirer as well as her sternest critic, was anxious that she do justice to her talent. When she was twenty, he urged her to submit some of her poems to the Pre-Raphaelite journal, *The Germ*. They appeared under the pseudonym Ellen Alleyn.

Dante Gabriel Rossetti (1828-1882) was the driving force of the Pre-Raphaelite Brotherhood, a group formed in 1848 under the influence of

John Ruskin. Also active in the movement were Gabriel's brother William Rossetti, Holman Hunt, Millais, and later Burne-Jones, William Morris, Swinburne, and others. Formed primarily to exchange ideas, the Pre-Raphaelites encouraged painting with the fidelity to nature and delicacy of treatment characteristic of Italian art before the time of Raphael. Their ideal was "true to nature."

Christina spent much time with these young, imaginative, hardworking people and from time to time served as their model, especially for Holman Hunt, who used her expression when he painted the face of Christ in *The Light of the World*.

As a painter, Dante Gabriel did not receive much formal training and showed little technical ability. He is noted chiefly as a colorist. He used Christina often as a model in his drawings and as the subject for the Virgin Mary in his best-known painting, *The Annunciation*.

In his book *Modern Art and the Death of a Culture*, Hans Rookmaaker said that the theology of the Pre-Raphaelites was not biblical but actually nineteenth-century liberalism—a romantic, overly sentimental movement that has affected English painting and writing ever since.

Dante Gabriel married the beautiful Elizabeth Siddal (painted by Millais for *Ophelia*). It was a quarrelsome marriage, although he loved to look at her beauty. She died two years later of an overdose of laudanum. Gabriel's grief was so extreme that he buried the manuscript of his current poems in her coffin. Nine years later, with his permission, they were exhumed.

One of Dante Gabriel's loveliest poems, "The Blessed Damozel," was set to music by Claude Debussy. It is the story of a transfigured woman leaning from "the gold bar of heaven" longing for her earthly lover to join her. One of the most beautiful songs the great English composer Vaughan Williams ever wrote is "Silent Noon," with words by Dante Gabriel.

When Mr. Rossetti's health began to fail, Frances gave French and Italian lessons to support the family. Christina was supposed to train to be a governess, but poor health prevented her. She told the poet Swinburne she was an "escaped governess."

Her brother William, who had prospered sufficiently to buy a home, invited the family to live with him soon after the father died. Christina was financially dependent on her brother for many years. She was grateful but still found this hard to accept.

Twice she refused to marry because her suitors did not share her religious convictions. James Collinson, a member of the Pre-Raphaelite Brotherhood, became a Roman Catholic. Charles Cayley, an agnostic scholar, had little faith. Both refusals pained Christina deeply.

In the poem "Another Spring," she described her dependent condition as a stinging comment on her life. However, in the words of one critic, "Her buoyant and tender soul was sharpened and refined by blow after blow of harsh discipline."

> *If I might see another spring,*
> *I'd not plant summer flowers and wait,*
> *I'd have my crocuses at once . . .*
> *Leaf-nested primroses; anything*
> *To blow at once, not late . . .*
> *If I might see another spring,*
> *I'd laugh today, today is brief;*
> *I would not wait for anything*
> *I'd use today that cannot last,*
> *Be glad today and sing.*

Christina considered her reputation as a poet as nothing compared to Dante Gabriel's, whose genius she thought would carry on the family name. Nevertheless, he urged her to prepare a volume of her poetry that he would illustrate.

In 1862 she published the book *Goblin Market and Other Poems*, and it was at once proclaimed outstanding. She was immediately recognized as a poet of charm, originality, and brilliance. *Goblin Market* is a fantasy about a girl's love for her sister. It describes temptation, resistance, and redemption. Like Jesus in the Christian Gospels, the redeeming figure, the sister Lizzie, participates in the sinful world but remains undefiled.

In 1872 Christina wrote *Sing-Song*, a much-loved collection of nursery rhymes for children. The title was suggested by her mother.

> *Who has seen the wind?*
> *Neither you nor I:*
> *But when the trees bow down their heads,*
> *The wind is passing by.*

Also from *Sing-Song:*

> *What are heavy? Sea—sand and sorrow;*
> *What are brief? Today and Tomorrow:*
> *What are frail? Spring blossoms and youth:*
> *What are deep? The ocean and truth.*

The writer Lewis Carroll, who was also an amateur photographer, took pictures of all five of the Rossettis, and he remained on cordial terms with Christina. Her *Goblin Market* inspired him to write *Alice's Adventures Underground*. He sent her a complimentary copy of *Alice in Wonderland*, which delighted her. Also interesting, Vincent Van Gogh quoted Christina's poem "Up-Hill" in one of his early sermons as a lay preacher in England.

In Christina's time feminist writers such as Harriet Martineau and Barbara Bodichon argued for professional employment for women in a variety of fields. Women should rely on themselves rather than depend on a father, brother, or husband. Christina did not become a feminist because she felt the movement was not guided by Scripture. She also declined to support women's suffrage.

Dependent on her brother for many years, she finally became self-supporting—to her great satisfaction. She said, "Money was a cheerer of spirits and a lightener of loads."

It is thought that Christina did her actual writing in the bedroom on the corner of the washstand. She worked in the home of her brother William for over forty years, and yet he never saw her in the act of composition.

When able, Christina helped her mother as well as several aunts, who also lived there, with domestic tasks. Of a nervous temperament, shy and reserved, Christina saved every free moment for writing. She did not cultivate sickness, but it sometimes freed her from unwelcome duties.

Several of her poems have become Christmas carols. "In the Bleak Mid-winter" describes the nativity scene in terms of the chilly English countryside. It is set to exquisite music by the noted English composer Gustav Holst.

> *In the bleak mid-winter*
> *Frosty wind made moan,*
> *Earth stood hard as iron,*
> *Water like a stone;*
> *Snow had fallen, snow on snow,*
> *Snow on snow*
> *In the bleak mid-winter*
> *Long ago.*

Other lovely Christmas songs by Christina are "Love Came Down at Christmas" and "Lo! New-Born Jesus, Soft and Weak and Small" (Jane Stuart Smith set the latter to music).

Christina's mother believed in the absolute and divine truth of everything found in the Old and New Testaments. Christina's sister Maria, a devout Christian, joined "All Saints Sisterhood." Whenever able, Christina occupied herself with Anglican church work, helping the poor. At one time she was a volunteer at the Highgate Penitentiary, comforting penitent young prostitutes.

Neither of her brothers were believers (Dante died of a drug overdose), which was a continual sorrow for Christina. She longed to see her loved ones in heaven someday. She often expressed the desire to escape the loneliness of this world for heaven.

In 1871 Christina was stricken with Grave's disease, which affected her appearance and endangered her life. She accepted her affliction with Christian courage and resignation and lived another twenty-three years, using what energy she had mainly for devotional writing. Like many creative people, she suffered ill health and yet had a deep capacity for joy. She wrote, "My heart is like a singing bird." Her poetry is chiefly lyrical and seems filled with music. Her diction is simple, original, and elegant.

Christina saw her poetic talent as a gift that came directly from God, that must not be squandered or forced. Although she never boasted of her creative powers, she knew she was a poet and a good one.

Biographer Eleanor W. Thomas said, "With such clear, strong faith, her poems often attain the luminous clarity and complete trust of George Herbert's." The language of the Bible is so dense in her poems as to go beyond quotation, being intrinsic to the structure of her verse. In childhood the Bible was part of her daily fare, and throughout her life she continued her close and attentive Bible study.

By the late nineteenth century, Christina's works were being compared to Elizabeth Barrett Browning's. Today "Christina Rossetti's poetry is more widely read and of keener interest to readers and critics than ever before," says Eleanor W. Thomas. This fact would be astonishing to the timid, modest Christina who "deprecated getting into paragraphs." Even when she was dying, she asked her church to pray for her but not to mention her name.

> *When I am dead, my dearest,*
> *Sing no sad songs for me.*

In her lifetime Christina Rossetti wrote over 900 poems in English and 60 in Italian. The majority of them are religious in subject and mood. Some of her books are a combination of poetry and prose, with simple but thought-provoking titles, such as *Called to be Saints, Time Flies,* and *Seek and Find.* Many of her poems express her profound love of nature.

Among the foremost poets of her time, Christina Rossetti made Christ the main focus of her life. She defines her faith in her beautiful hymn "None Other Lamb":

> *None other Lamb, none other name,*
> *None other hope in Heav'n or earth or sea.*
> *None other hiding place from guilt and shame,*
> *None beside Thee.*
>
> *My faith burns low, my hope burns low;*
> *Only my heart's desire cries out in me*
> *By the deep thunder of its want and woe,*
> *Cries out to Thee.*

> Lord, Thou art life, though I be dead;
> Love's fire Thou art, however cold I be:
> Nor Heav'n have I, nor place to lay my head,
> Nor home, but Thee.

Christina Rossetti was indeed a great saint and a great poet.

BIBLIOGRAPHY

Marsh, Jan. *Christina Rossetti: A Writer's Life*. New York: Viking Penguin, 1995.

Rossetti, Christina. *Christina Rossetti's Poems*. Boston: Roberts Brothers, 1895.

Thomas, Frances. *Christina Rossetti*. London: Virago Press Ltd., 1994.

RECOMMENDED READING

Goblin Market and Other Poems
Sing-Song
A Birthday
Remember
A Summer Wish
Twilight Calm
The Lowest Place
Paradise

DOROTHY L. SAYERS

1893-1957

The Christian faith is the most exciting drama that ever
staggered the imagination of man. . . .

Dorothy L. Sayers

Dorothy L. Sayers was one of the most brilliant and fascinating women of the twentieth century. She was earnest, hard-working, deeply religious, witty, scholarly, generous, and kind, though she could also be rude, impatient, and eccentric. She was a woman who knew her own mind and was certain it was as good as any man's. All her life she had been aware of a strong urge to create, and she did so with great gusto and joy. A whirlwind of activity in her sixty-four years, she produced with intense intellectual ardor a remarkable body of work.

Dorothy was born in Oxford where her father, an Anglican minister, was head of the choir school at Christ Church. He was not only a good musician but also a classic scholar who taught Latin to the young choir boys. Dorothy was strongly influenced by her kind father, who filled her life with books and ideas. Realizing that she was extremely bright, he began teaching her Latin when she was seven. He soon found she had an amazing gift for languages. He affectionately called her his "little humbug."

She grew up in a home where books were all about. She read everything she could get her hands on, and whatever she read, she thought about and remembered. She knew children's classics and often quoted from them in her later writings. Books were her friends in a sometimes lonely life. Because of her love of reading, she decided at an early age that she wanted to be a writer and never changed her mind.

When her father was offered a better position, the family moved to the rectory at Bluntisham, England, in the Fens Parish, when Dorothy was four. The flatlands of the Fens often flooded; sometimes the whole countryside was covered with water as harsh winds swept down from the North Sea. It was called "the attack of the North Sea." In the bleak, isolated Fens, life was lonely, and the rectory, though large, was somewhat primitive and cold. However, there was room for her parents, Grandmother Sayers, Aunt Maud Leigh, Dorothy's nursemaid, and servants.

As an only child, she was used to being the center of attention and enjoyed it. Though she was often alone, she was close to her cousin Ivy Shrimpton, who was later to play a key role in her life. Usually with adults, Dorothy (whose name means "gift of God") was talked to as an adult. When she appeared downstairs (like Beatrix Potter, she and her nursemaid lived on the top floor), she was not to speak unless spoken to.

High-spirited and mischievous, she had a delightful sense of humor. Among her most vivid recollections of her childhood was a walk with her nursemaid when they spied in a dentist's front window two rows of false teeth that slowly opened and closed.

Her daily life was bound up with the religious duties of a minister's family. Later in her writing she depicted clergymen as kind and available in trouble but absent-minded. Dorothy was thoroughly familiar with three great treasures of the English language—*The Book of Common Prayer* written by Bishop Cranmer, the King James version of the Bible, and the plays of Shakespeare.

She regularly attended church, and although she went through a time of questioning as an adolescent, she remained a practicing Christian. As we shall see, Dorothy became a staunch defender of orthodox Christianity, understanding that history is all of one piece and that the Bible is an integral part of it. She early developed a feeling for the past and its relationship to the present.

At that time most fathers did not educate their daughters the way they did their sons. Girls usually stayed at home and were educated by governesses and by their own reading in preparation for marriage. England did not have compulsory education before 1870 and had no public high schools until 1902. Fortunately Dorothy had parents who were amazingly generous and supportive. They early planned for her university education and sent her away to boarding school at age sixteen.

Here at Godolphin, in the strict evangelical atmosphere, she did not care for the rules. She was neither pretty nor popular, but she was a good scholar. Students called her "Swanny" because of her long neck. As a result of extreme nearsightedness, she had to wear glasses or squint. However, due to her determination to learn, she won one of the highest scholarships in England and entered Somerville College at Oxford in 1912. For her it was like coming home.

Oxford is England's oldest university, located in a beautiful medieval town with storybook architecture that always inspired Dorothy. The university is made up of independent colleges with groups of buildings joined by a formal central courtyard. Each college has its own chapel, library, and dining room where students live and learn. Oxford has been the home of many famous persons, including Roger Bacon, John Wycliffe, and Lewis Carroll. The Oxford University Press is also located there.

Dorothy studied in Oxford's oldest library, the Bodleian, and often in her energetic, enthusiastic manner talked out loud, disturbing other scholars.

Always full of zest for her studies, Dorothy loved her three years at Somerville. They helped to shape her adult personality. She sang in the famous Oxford Bach choir and quickly fell in love with the conductor, to the amusement of her classmates.

She wore outlandish clothes and took part in amateur theatricals, as she had a lifelong love for the theater. Ever ready for a debate, Dorothy and some of her friends started the Mutual Admiration Society (MAS) where women writers gathered to discuss their work. Several remained her lifetime friends. The group was somewhat similar to the Inklings, started by C. S. Lewis, Charles Williams, and J. R. R. Tolkien. Dorothy herself was never an Inkling because women were not allowed to join. In later years these women referred to the MAS as the Middle Age Spread. In all the ups and downs of Dorothy's life, her saving grace was a sense of humor.

In her Oxford years she was influenced by G. K. Chesterton (1874-1936), who played a major part in London literary life for almost forty years. He wrote essays, biographies, and, of particular interest to Dorothy, a series of mysteries featuring a character named Father Brown. Like Chesterton, she believed it made more sense to be orthodox than a heretic. One of her favorite topics to debate was Christianity. Dorothy felt a lifelong gratitude for Chesterton, who was a kind of unconventional Christian liberator whom she later knew personally.

Dorothy believed that Oxford was sacred in the world of ideas. Among her fond memories were the sound of tower bells and the exquisite architecture, which figure in her novel about college life, *Gaudy Night*. In this novel Somerville appears as Shrewsbury College, and Dorothy expresses her nostalgia for the academic life. When she completed her course of study, she was sad to leave her studies, her tutor Miss Pope, and her friends. She was graduated with First Class honors in Modern Languages and was one of the first women to be awarded an Oxford degree.

"The hatred of work must be one of the most depressing consequences of the Fall," wrote Dorothy. She never failed to give every ounce of energy and enthusiasm in her work of getting an education. Already determined to be a writer, she needed to find a way of supporting herself while writing. She tried teaching but found it too demanding.

Meanwhile, in 1916, when she was twenty-three, her first volume of poetry, called *OPI*, was published in Oxford. Neither that nor her second volume sold well. Finally in 1922, unable to make a living from her scholarship or her poetry, she took a job at Benson's in London and became one of the few women to be employed writing advertising copy. Her father continued to give her a small allowance to help pay the rent. She was good at her job and stayed at it for nine years.

Dorothy is credited with inventing the slogan, "It pays to advertise." She gained a reputation for being merry, talkative, and always ready to jump into an argument over ideas. A night owl, she often worked late and expected too much of everybody, including herself. She operated in a masculine work world and proved herself equal.

Until after the First World War, detective stories were nearly all written by men. Dorothy became an authority on detective fiction, and she especially admired Bentley's *Trent's Last Case* and Sherlock Holmes. She believed that detective stories are among the most moral literature, because crime is always punished, although she wondered if these stories gave weak people ideas for crime.

One of her chief claims to fame was her creation of Lord Peter Wimsey, one of the more complicated amateur detectives in mystery fiction. Very wealthy, Lord Peter was enthusiastic about music, old books, and cricket. He first appeared in 1923 in the novel *Whose Body?* Like most beginning authors, Dorothy had trouble finding a publisher, so the book was printed in America. It was not a bestseller, but soon an English publisher brought out her second mystery, *Clouds of Witnesses.*

Other prominent characters in the series of Wimsey novels are Lord Wimsey's clever valet Bunter, Parker of Scotland Yard, and Harriet Vane, who later marries Peter. By now Dorothy had several hobbies—crossword puzzles, photography, and riding a motorcycle—which appear in her books.

She was clever, amusing, tall, and plain. When her hair fell out after an illness, she wore a silver wig for years, along with large earrings and startling clothes. She had beautiful artistic hands, wore a ring on every finger, and smoked cigarettes in a long holder. Dorothy was a big, impressive woman with strong opinions that she voiced loudly. She was always upset if her middle initial *L* (Leigh) was left out. It was her mother's maiden name.

Dorothy fell in love with several men. John Cournos, a Russian Jew, abandoned her to marry someone else, leaving her in turmoil. In 1924, when she was thirty years old, she had a son by Bill White, born out of wedlock. This was kept a close secret, even from her parents, until her death. She realized that the scandal might ruin her writing career. She later believed that sex outside of marriage was a bitter sin, for which she had suffered.

Dorothy did not have an abortion nor put her son up for adoption because she loved him and wanted him. Her favorite cousin, Ivy Shrimpton, took him into her home, where he lived for the first ten years of his life. Later he came to live with Dorothy after she married Mac Fleming. Dorothy went often to visit John Anthony, who thought she was his aunt. She believed it was her job alone to support her son. So she worked hard, like a human dynamo, and always financed his needs, including a fine education later. In her last will, she left him almost everything.

In 1926 she married Mac Fleming, a divorced man twelve years her senior. She simply announced her marriage to her family, who accepted him, especially her favorite Aunt Maud, who later lived with the Flemings until her death.

Mac was an attractive Scotsman, a captain in the Army Service Corps. But war in the trenches had caused him to suffer from depression, so eventually he was unable to work, and Dorothy supported both of them.

The more successful she became, the more difficult their life together must have been. He spent hours drinking at a local pub and resented being called Dorothy Sayers's husband, although he was proud of her. She was very protective of him and in the early years enjoyed his company, for they both had a zest for life. He died suddenly of a stroke in 1950. A comment he had made previously showed his state of mind: He would be "glad to be out of it all."

Dorothy had left her advertising job in 1931 in order to do full-time writing and lecturing. She had decided that advertising manipulated people to buy things they didn't need or want. Because she needed money, she wrote continually. She hated being interrupted during her precious times of creativity. Being a perfectionist, she knew that writing requires long hours of concentration and that one must work at the craft daily. She did a lot of her writing in handsome longhand on cheap paper-covered children's exercise books.

Untidy in her working habits and now grossly overweight, she and her bedroom and study usually looked a mess. When working on a writing project, she took walks up and down her garden or did jigsaw puzzles. Through all her trials she stuck to her job of writing. Afraid to trust her emotions, she found security only in her work. However there was always a lighter side to Dorothy's nature in spite of her worst moments, and her sense of fun was irrepressible.

In 1936 Dorothy was asked to write a play similar to T. S. Eliot's famous *Murder in the Cathedral* for the Canterbury Cathedral. She responded by writing *The Zeal of Thy House* and had a marvelous time helping with the production. She loved the theater and said she found there the kind of community the church is meant to be.

Now her direction changed as she was awakened to the dramatic power of the Christian truths that were to dominate her thinking for years to come. She said that the creeds claimed that Jesus in fact and in truth was the God by whom the universe was made. She insisted that "the doctrine really was that Christ was always and equally God and man." She understood that the doctrine of the Trinity is basic to Christianity.

Because of her detective novels, Dorothy was often asked to speak on crime and Christianity. An adolescent commented, "And then there was Miss Dorothy Sayers who turned from a life of crime to join the Church of England."

By 1937 Dorothy was a celebrity. Good about writing to her fans, she kept up a huge correspondence in longhand, including letters to C. S. Lewis and Charles Williams. Friendship was one of the most important features of her life, more reliable than marriage, more lasting than sex. She was linked to her friends by a vast network of letters and by work shared.

Her household always included a cat or cats. She liked the animals because of their native pride and independence. In her Witham home she maintained a room where neighboring cats came to have kittens, which she took in a taxi to London restaurants as mousers. During the Second World War, she kept pigs and chickens for food but was always upset at slaughter time, as the animals were like family pets.

In 1938 Dorothy was asked by the BBC to write a series of radio plays on the life of Christ. "Being a Christian became an intellectual adventure, one that she pursued with all her heart and with all her soul, and with all her mind." As a biblical scholar, she said that the life of Christ was the turning point in history: "The man we hanged on the cross was God Almighty."

The church needed Dorothy Sayers as a fresh defender. Both Dorothy and C. S. Lewis gave many radio talks "in defense of Christianity." C. S. Lewis's talks were later published as *Mere Christianity*. Another defender of the faith, T. S. Eliot, said after war was declared on September 6, 1939: "We had before us the alternative of Christianity or paganism." Dorothy wrote a letter to *The Times* urging that churches be kept open during the war even if theaters had to be closed. She was a strong patriot with conservative political views.

In 1944 she wrote her book *The Mind of the Maker*, concerning the nature of creativity as a demonstration of the image of God. God as a maker and artist has given human beings this creative ability. Dorothy became more and more interested in creativity and believed we are most alive when using this power. "God took pleasure in creation . . . if we want to know what the mind of the Creator is, we must look at Christ."

She called God the "Master Builder" and noted, "Man is like God in the ability to create, and to him creation is another name for work." Dorothy believed artistic work was a sacramental act and that one is responsible for one's abilities. Her own sense of responsibility was titanic, and she continued to work furiously.

The radio series, *The Man Born to Be King*, about the kingship of Christ, was her masterpiece. A great triumph for her personally in spite of theological criticism, it was a national success. She wrote that man is a fallen creature but able to choose between good and evil.

In 1951 in her play *The Emperor Constantine*, she described

Constantine's conversion, an event that helped to make Christianity a great earthly power. (It was Constantine who convened the renowned Council of Nicea, which stood for biblical orthodoxy and insisted on the divine/human nature of Christ.) As usual Dorothy was involved in the production.

Never a militant feminist, she was still a defender of women and their rights. She wrote witty essays on the role of women in society, published with the title *Are Women Human?*

What she valued most was a love of learning for its own sake. A constant reader, she bought many books and delighted in losing herself in a scholarly piece of research. She had already translated *The Song of Roland* and *Tristan in Brittany* from medieval French. Now with the energy of a well-stocked mind, she taught herself medieval Italian in order to translate Dante's *The Divine Comedy*. Dorothy became a Dante scholar and lecturer, seeking to introduce him to the modern world. She found humor in his work and thought that his poetry was built like a great Gothic cathedral. Dorothy Sayers insisted that an author cannot "die" as long as his or her work exists.

Living on royalties while translating Dante became increasingly difficult. Because of her lectures on Dante, she became a close friend with her biographer, Barbara Reynolds, an Italian scholar and translator. Reynolds later completed Sayers's translation of *The Divine Comedy*.

After an extremely active and intellectual life, Dorothy suddenly died of heart failure as she was going downstairs to feed her hungry cats. She was sixty-four.

She had expressed to her colleague Val Gielgud, "When we go to Heaven, all I ask is that we shall be given some interesting job and allowed to get on with it. No management; no box office; no dramatic critics; and an audience of cheerful angels who don't mind laughing."

A memorial at her beloved Somerville College in Oxford reads, "Praise Him that He hath made man in His own image, a Maker and craftsman like Himself."

BIBLIOGRAPHY

Dale, Alzina Stone. *Maker and Craftsman: The Story of Dorothy L. Sayers.* Grand Rapids: Eerdmans Publishing Co., 1978.

Reynolds, Barbara. *Dorothy L. Sayers: Her Life and Soul.* New York: St. Martin's Press, 1993.

RECOMMENDED READING

Lord Peter Views the Body
Gaudy Night
Murder Must Advertise
The Nine Tailors
The Man Born to Be King
The Mind of the Maker

GERTRUDE STEIN

1874-1946

I want to be historical.

Gertrude Stein

Gertrude Stein's strong statement, "Simplify, simplify!" is well illustrated in one of her famous lines, "A rose is a rose is a rose is a rose."

In her lifetime she was the center of bitter controversy. Some ridiculed her as a literary fraud—a rich, talkative, egotistical dilettante convinced of her own genius. The critics accused her of being the high priestess of the "cult of unintelligibility."

Others admired her originality and believed she had brought about a one-woman revolution—that she was one of the century's most radical innovators. As the focus of this argument, she became well known in Paris among other writers, painters, musicians, and photographers. She was one of the first to realize the significance of various experimental movements such as cubism. Her career was dedicated to unorthodoxy.

Born into an affluent German-Jewish family in Allegheny, Pennsylvania, she spent her early years in Vienna and Paris where she learned several languages. In later years she insisted that she was not interested in anything but English.

Her unhappy adolescent years were spent in Oakland, California. It was a lonely time, except for the companionship of her brother Leo, her favorite sibling. She was not fond of her parents. Her demanding father had a harsh temper, and her mother was weak and shallow. Gertrude was a high school dropout, and she filled her solitary hours by devouring books indiscriminately. She remembered going through whole libraries reading anything, everything, especially detective stories.

She commented once that her father, who never read a book, died "fat and fishing." After the death of both parents, she moved to Baltimore at the age of eighteen to live with relatives. Her new family was large and prosperous, so she was no longer lonely but rather charmed and fascinated with her new life. Her brother Michael had taken over family affairs and with his business ingenuity was able to provide small independent incomes for his brother and sisters.

With Leo at Harvard, Gertrude attended Radcliffe College where she studied psychology under the well-known philosopher William James. His influence on her writing was enduring—stimulating her experimentation with words and ideas. She was interested in contemporary ideas and exposed to evolution.

In her last year at Radcliffe, she wrote on her final exam papers, "Dear Professor James, I am so sorry, but I do not feel a bit like an examination on philosophy today." James wrote in reply, "I understand perfectly. I often feel like that myself." He gave her the highest mark in the class. Gertrude's writing was also influenced by William's brother, Henry James.

When Gertrude was twenty-three, she entered Johns Hopkins School of Medicine and studied there for four years. Here she became lifelong friends with Claribel and Etta Cone. Although her work was excellent, she left without taking a degree. She was more interested in study than high marks and finally decided that she was thoroughly bored with medicine. However, she later applied her study of the brain to the arts of painting and writing.

In 1903 Gertrude settled in Paris with her brother Leo at 27 rue de Fleurus, in the artists' Quartier Montparnasse. Her brother Michael and his wife, Sarah, also lived in Paris and had become art collectors. Michael and Sarah were the first to bring a Matisse painting to the

United States. Later Michael's French home was designed by the great Swiss architect Le Corbusier. Continually visiting art galleries and attending the theater, Leo and Gertrude began meeting people and attracting visitors to their home.

At first it was Leo who, through his contact in Florence with the famous art critic Bernard Berenson, introduced Gertrude to important painters such as Cezanne. Together Gertrude and Leo began buying modern paintings before the artists' names were well known. The Steins were able to acquire inexpensively works by Cezanne, Gauguin, Renoir, Picasso, Matisse, Braque, Gris, and so on. She told Ernest Hemingway, "You can either buy clothes or buy pictures. It's that simple."

More and more people came to see the paintings, discuss aesthetics, and hammer out fresh ideas. As the Steins were hospitable and talkative, 27 rue de Fleurus (sometimes called the first modern art gallery) became a gathering place, especially on Saturday nights, for an amazing variety of painters, writers, musicians such as Erik Satie, and photographers such as Man Ray.

Picasso brought to the "art gallery" the French cubist poet Max Jacob and the notables Apollinaire, Marie Laurencin, Braque, Derain, Delaunay, and Henri Rousseau. These were the rebels of the new century. Picasso and Gertrude immediately understood each other, and he became a "soul mate and brother in the arts."

Gertrude's first publication in 1896, "Normal Motor Automatism," had been the result of her investigation of automatic writing. By 1904 at the age of thirty, she had not only become an art critic and collector, but she had begun writing books. As there was a steady flow of visitors at rue de Fleurus, she waited until all had left and then began writing at 11 P.M. through the night until just before dawn.

Looking at a Cezanne painting as her inspiration, she wrote *Three Lives* in 1905. Lack of a publisher never deterred Gertrude. She simply continued to pile up manuscripts. She wrote something every day under any circumstances, even if she had only half an hour or was in her automobile Godiva. She had much to do, and she did it with deep conviction, eventually completing a monumental body of work

Short and of massive, square proportions, with an androgynous nature, she reminded Ernest Hemingway of an Italian peasant woman, and her style of dress in corduroy he called "strange steerage clothes." Later when her companion Alice Toklas cut her hair, Hemingway said she looked like a Roman Caesar.

Gertrude was an independent woman with her own income, small as it was, but it freed her from the burden of finding a job. She loved books, and she enjoyed knowing a lot of people. Everyone was fascinated by her charm and intelligence. She had an expansive personality, an explosive temper, an amusing sense of humor, and a hardy laugh that came straight from her heart. She was a legend in her day. She was serenely and maddeningly herself. A person of great energy, she loved to walk about Paris with her dog Basket, creating sentences to write down later.

Gertrude had a never-failing curiosity. She was original and eccentric, yet her common sense and honesty in conversation gained her high respect for her opinions, although few people claimed to read her writing. With a strong will to dominate, she at one time had enormous prestige.

In 1906 Picasso painted a stunning portrait of Gertrude Stein—now in the Metropolitan Museum of Art in New York. After nearly ninety sittings, he erased her face and painted on what looks like an African mask. "But I don't look like this!" Gertrude exclaimed. Picasso replied, "You will." It was during her modeling for this painting that she started to write her mammoth novel *The Making of Americans*.

In 1907 Picasso, influenced by African sculpture, painted *Les Demoiselles d'Avignon*. The first masterpiece of cubism, it broke decisively with the art of the past and marked the birth of modern art. In this same year Gertrude met Alice B. Toklas. Alice later said that she had met only three geniuses in her life, and each time a bell within her rang. The three were Gertrude Stein, Pablo Picasso, and the English philosopher Alfred Whitehead.

In 1910 Alice came to live with Gertrude at 27 rue de Fleurus, and this was a lasting, happy relationship until Gertrude's death in 1946. Totally loyal, they were an enormous help to each other and were never apart for thirty-nine years. Alice was secretary, companion, shopper, and gourmet cook. In a sense, she regulated Gertrude's life, becoming the power behind the throne. Because of Alice, Gertrude was freed from all domestic chores and could concentrate on her writing and on being a genius. Alice always said that Gertrude was the writer, and she was the maid servant.

Gertrude said, "It takes a lot of time to be a genius. You have to sit around so much doing nothing, really doing nothing." As she wrote in her charming book *Everybody's Autobiography,* "It is quite true what is known as work is something that I cannot do; it makes me nervous. I can read and write, and I can wander around, and I can drive an automobile, and I can talk, and that is almost all; doing anything else makes me nervous."

Gertrude and Alice were "dear enemies," as Gertrude delighted in saying teasingly. For example, Alice prepared superb meals and liked her food hot, so Gertrude would find every excuse to linger until the meals were cold. Alice had the intellectual brilliance to appreciate Gertrude's mind. Without Alice there may never have been a Gertrude.

Gertrude's handwriting was almost illegible, so her friend Etta Cone typed her first book, *Three Lives. The Autobiography of Alice B. Toklas* describes what happened: "*Three Lives* had been typewritten and now the next thing was to show it to a publisher. Someone gave Gertrude the name of an agent in New York, and she tried that. Nothing came of it. Then she tried publishers directly. . . . This attempt to find a publisher lasted some time, and then without being really discouraged, she decided to [pay to] have it printed. It was not an unnatural thought as people often did this in Paris." (And many other places.) Gertrude was thirty-five at the time. *Three Lives* is considered by critics to be among her best works.

Claribel and Etta Cone, Gertrude's Baltimore friends, became life-long art collectors. Their remarkable collection is now displayed in a Baltimore art museum. Whenever Gertrude needed money, she would sell the Cone sisters a Cezanne, a Picasso drawing, or other art works she had accumulated, thus saving them the middleman's fee.

Leo disapproved of Gertrude's writing and her interest in Picasso; nor was he happy with Alice's presence. He had become aggressive, neurotic, and self-centered. An endless talker, he achieved little. Gertrude refused to be dominated by a man who was brilliant, erratic, and unfulfilled. With mounting tension between them, they finally broke off their relationship after almost forty years.

Leo said, "Gertrude and I are just the contrary. She's basically stupid, and I'm basically intelligent." They divided their art collection and never saw each other again, although Leo continued to criticize his sister from a distance. This was 1913, the year of the Armory Show in New York. With "New Spirit" as its motto, this art exhibit was the great demarcation point between traditional art and the modern art of the twentieth century. The show met with derision in spite of its masterpieces. Gertrude Stein came to be identified with these artists, especially the Fauvists and Cubists.

Alice took Leo's place in Gertrude's life, and the two friends became endlessly hospitable. Gertrude talked to their male guests, and Alice talked to the wives of some of these geniuses. Irrepressible themselves, these two women were at the cultural heart of Paris for four decades in their art gallery/salon.

Gertrude and Alice remained in France during the First and Second World Wars. Although expatriates, they loved America and so did strenuous work for the soldiers in both wars. They distributed food and medicine under harsh conditions, visited the wounded in hospitals, and spent large sums of their own money on soldiers and their families, sometimes seriously overdrawing their bank account. In her book *Wars I Have Seen*, Gertrude said that these were her happiest years.

The two women discovered the beauty of the Rhone Valley, and so for seventeen consecutive years they spent six months of the year at Belley and Bilignin. Here Gertrude was as prolific as ever. During the Second World War, they were urged to leave the country because they were Jews, but they decided to remain in Bilignin. They got to know ordinary French people with whom the main topic of conversation was the shortage of butter and gasoline. Soldiers delighted in them because of their generosity and vivid personalities.

As a patron of the arts as well as a poet, playwright, and novelist, Gertrude was called "The Mother of Modernism." Others spoke of her as the "Mother Goose" of Montparnasse—"Yet a goose with a mind." She eagerly courted publicity, thrived on company, and lived to enjoy her own controversial literary celebrity.

She originated the phrase, "The Lost Generation" and had a strong influence on Ernest Hemingway, although their friendship ended badly as she objected to his growing obsession with sex and violent death. His excessive drinking and depression finally led him to suicide.

Others she influenced were Sherwood Anderson, F. Scott Fitzgerald, Stephen Crane, and Thornton Wilder, who were seeking new ways of expression. She was especially close to Sherwood Anderson. He considered her a pathfinder and said, "She dared, in the face of ridicule and misunderstanding, to try to waken in all of us who write, a new feeling for words." On the other hand James Joyce disliked her and said, "I hate intellectual women." T. S. Eliot deplored her influence.

Encouraged by William James, she invented "Steinese," a literary idiom that became a scandal and a delight. An example: "Pigeons in the grass, alas!" (from *Four Saints in Three Acts*) or the title of one of her books, *Before the Flowers of Friendship Faded Friendship Faded*. She was always trying to do a new thing in a new way. "Why do something if it can be done?" she reasoned.

Her writing became daring and difficult as she worked on a high plane of creative thinking. As Picasso tried to do in color and images, she sought to portray in words, "not what you see, but what you know is there."

She insisted on the artist's need to be contemporary and pressed for a continuing revitalization of the language: "Simplify, simplify." Much repetition with variants and little punctuation was basic to her style. She felt it more important to reveal the feeling of a character than to tell a story.

Absolutely committed to Picasso, she was one of the first supporters of Cubism. Another champion of the movement was the poet Guillaume Apollinaire, who became the Cubist movement's chief publicist.

Gertrude wrote a series of "portraits" of people, including Cezanne, Matisse, and Picasso, which are early examples of her difficult work. She attempted to do in words what painters did in painting. Her dear friend Carl Van Vechten had launched Gertrude's publishing career by having *Tender Buttons* printed. The book, strongly influenced by the Cubism of Picasso and Braque, was abstract like their paintings.

By the time she wrote *Tender Buttons,* there was no longer anything in the English language with which her work might be compared. She believed that her fragmentary style reflected the disintegrating spirit of the age. This reminds one of Francis Schaeffer's deep concern over the fragmentation of twentieth-century society in his book *How Should We Then Live?*

As Gertrude continued to pile up unpublished manuscripts, Alice typed them, and they decided to take a further step. Together they started a publishing company in 1931, called it Plain Edition, and paid to have Gertrude's writings printed.

Finally, in exasperation Alice urged Gertrude to write something that made money. In response Gertrude wrote *The Autobiography of Alice B. Toklas* in six weeks, an extraordinary feat. This highly amusing book, written in an understandable style, was published in England in 1933. It was an immediate top seller and is now considered one of the best memoirs in American literature. This first real success came at age fifty-nine.

Gertrude enjoyed making money for the first time in her life. She commented, "Money is funny." She proved to be a woman of immense purpose, equipped with astonishing powers of concentration and hard work. She knew also how to relax—by reading detective stories and walking many, many miles. On picnics she liked to lie in the sun and stare right into it. "This clears my mind," she said.

In 1935, after thirty years away from the United States, Gertrude had a highly successful lecture tour in many key cities. She was a legend, and people flocked to hear and see her. She describes these events amusingly in her book *Everyone's Autobiography*.

She would say, "It's interesting," or "It's not interesting," when expressing her strong opinions. She loved long sentences and paragraphs, which sometimes ended with "anyway."

In Brinnin's excellent biography of Gertrude, he comments, "Even her admirers despair when they must account for the discrepancy between the canny, wise and deeply erudite cast of her mind and spoken words, and the vast wastes of utter 'thoughtlessness' which are the most of her written words."

While in the United States, Gertrude attended the opera *Four Saints in Three Acts*, which she had written, with music by Virgil Thomson. Her other opera, *The Mother of Us All*, also with music by Thomson, is based on the life of Susan B. Anthony, who helped win the women's right to vote. Brinnin said about *The Mother of Us All*, "At the very end of her life [Gertrude] had written one of her most powerful and beautiful works."

After returning to Paris, Gertrude was in great demand. Always making new friends, she had an insatiable need to be "talking and listening" at the same time, with seemingly endless vitality. She had rarely been ill, nor did she trust doctors and medicine, but now she began to fail physically. She was diagnosed with incurable cancer and suddenly hospitalized in Paris.

She decided on a dangerous operation with little hope of success. She said to Alice, "One has to learn everything, even dying." Then she added sadly, "What is the answer?" She had never found a reply to satisfy her. "In that case," she said quietly, "what is the question?" Gertrude sank into a coma and died soon afterward. She is buried in the famous Père-Lachaise Cemetery in Paris.

Early in her life Gertrude had read the Bible to learn about eternity. "There was nothing there," she said. "There was God, of course, and He spoke, but there was nothing about eternity." How tragic that she missed God's marvelous promise of eternal life. As it says in John 3:16: "For God so loved the world that He gave his only begotten Son, that whosoever believeth in Him should not perish but have everlasting life." And there is Job's triumphant statement, "For I know that my Redeemer liveth and that He shall stand at the latter day upon the earth; and though worms destroy this body, yet in my flesh shall I see God."

Although Gertrude left the bulk of her estate to Alice, because of family greed Gertrude's lifelong companion had little money or comfort and was hardly able to pay her bills. In her cold, lonely apartment she said, "I keep to the radiator." However, she was able to write two charming books: *The Alice B. Toklas Cookbook* and *What Is Remembered*.

Alice was eventually drawn to Christianity and converted to Roman Catholicism. She said, "Now I have everything to learn to live in the peace of our Lord Jesus Christ." Broke and bedridden, she lived to be almost ninety. She died in 1967 and is buried close to Gertrude.

Gertrude affirmed, from her earliest days on, that she had always wanted to make history. And that she surely has!

BIBLIOGRAPHY

Brinnin, John Malcolm. *The Third Rose: Gertrude Stein and Her World.* Boston: Little, Brown and Company, 1959.

Stein, Gertrude. *Selected Writings of Gertrude Stein.* New York: Random House, Inc., 1945.

Stendhal, Renate, ed. *Gertrude Stein in Words and Pictures.* Chapel Hill, N.C.: Algonquin Books of Chapel Hill, 1994.

RECOMMENDED READING

Three Lives
The Autobiography of Alice B. Toklas
Everybody's Autobiography
Wars I Have Seen

HARRIET BEECHER STOWE

1811-1896

So this is the little lady who
made this big war!

Abraham Lincoln

In describing herself Harriet Beecher Stowe wrote, "I am a little bit of a woman—somewhat more than forty, about as thin and dry as a pinch of snuff, never very much to look at in my best days and looking like a used-up article now." Yet she had become one of the most talked-about women in the world after the publication of her remarkable novel *Uncle Tom's Cabin*.

Harriet Beecher was born on June 14, 1811, in Litchfield, Connecticut. Her father, Lyman Beecher, was one of the most powerful Puritan preachers of his generation in America, having been influenced by the great theologian Jonathan Edwards. Harriet was the daughter, sister, wife, and mother of preachers.

She was the seventh child in an exuberantly evangelical household. Under Lyman Beecher's dynamic preaching, genuine revival came to his congregation. He spoke out strongly against Unitarians and liberals, insisting on the inspired truth of the Bible. In his home lively theological discussions took place after the reading aloud of great literature such as John Milton's *Paradise Lost*.

Harriet's mother, a devout Christian, died when Harriet was four years old. As Mrs. Beecher was dying, her last prayer was that all her sons might be called to the ministry. This prayer was answered in years to come. The youngest son, Henry Ward Beecher, became the greatest minister of his time.

Harriet often heard her father read the Bible in an eager tone of admiring delight and expectancy, as if the book had just been handed to him out of heaven. She had a bright mind and a remarkable memory. When she was six, she could read well and had memorized over twenty-five hymns and two long chapters from the Bible.

She did not care for her strict, somber stepmother but spent happy hours reading good books in her father's library. She became a Christian during a Communion service. When she told her father, he said, "There has a new flower blossomed in the kingdom of heaven this day." She became one of the most Christ-centered women the United States has ever produced.

Harriet was sent to the academy in Litchfield, where her father taught the Bible and accordingly received free tuition for his children. At age thirteen she attended the Female Seminary in Hartford, Connecticut, founded by her sisters Catharine and Mary. Later Harriet also became a member of the faculty. She was an avid reader and especially appreciated Sir Walter Scott and Lord Byron. In her youth she was already interested in a writing career.

In 1832, at the age of twenty, Harriet moved with her family to Cincinnati, Ohio, when her father became president of Lane Theological Seminary. Her best friend Eliza was married to Calvin Stowe, a member of the Lane faculty and a leading authority on the Bible. After Eliza's sudden death in 1836, Calvin and Harriet married because of their mutual love for Eliza.

At age thirty-three Calvin was stocky, near-sighted, and bald, with a large beard all over his face. He was a hypochondriac and fond of overeating. Eventually he became enormously fat and grew childishly helpless. When Harriet married him, Calvin was apparently the only man who had ever shown any interest in her. They had seven children and lived in cramped poverty. She remarked, "Calvin Stowe is rich in knowledge and, alas, rich in nothing else."

The nursery and kitchen were the principal fields of labor for Harriet. Fortunately she had a sense of humor. When Calvin was away in a sanatorium because of ill health, he wrote depressing letters of his being "all but dead." She commented, "I read the letter and poke it into the fire and proceed."

In order to earn money to support her family, Harriet began writing stories and articles for journals and magazines. Although Calvin had a brilliant mind, part of the time he was incapable of making a living. She wrote continually, when possible, as the problems and anxieties of running the home fell on her shoulders.

She wrote about temperance and the evils of dancing and the theater. In her many tales of New England history, she sought to make clear the positive and negative sides of Puritanism. As a Calvinist, Harriet believed that whenever Calvin's system of theology disappeared, civil liberty would disappear with it. Then under the influence of her brother, the famous Henry Ward Beecher who preached against slavery, she began to describe the horrors of the slave trade, calling it a national sin. In 1845 she wrote a story appealing to the South to free their slaves. Ironically, she herself often felt a slave to family cares, household chores, and ill health.

In Ohio she became aware of the Underground Railroad, an informal system that helped slaves escape to the northern states and Canada during the mid-1800s. It was neither underground nor a railroad. Railroad terms were used as codes. For example, hiding places were called stations, and those who helped were called conductors. Slaves traveled at night, often through Ohio, Indiana, and Pennsylvania, and hid in the daytime. The Quakers, especially Levi Coffin, helped thousands to escape. Harriet Tubman, a runaway slave herself, was another well-known "conductor."

In 1850 the Fugitive Slave Law made it a criminal act to assist runaway slaves and also provided for the return of fugitives. Heavy penalties were imposed on people who aided slaves to escape. Both Thomas Jefferson and Patrick Henry had earlier spoken out strongly against slavery. But Harriet's contemporaries—Longfellow, Hawthorne, Alcott, Emerson, Melville, Thoreau, Dickinson, and Whittier—did not act, even though they loathed slavery. Even Harriet's father did not stand up with the abolitionists.

Harriet analyzed the issue of slavery during the days of the Fugitive Slave Law. She was horrified by her investigation and determined to write something to expose the cruelty of slavery, which she considered a cancer on society. Around this time she received a letter from her sister-in-law Isabella: "Hattie, if I could use a pen as you can, I would write something that will make this whole nation feel what an accursed thing slavery is."

Harriet's response was, "As long as the baby sleeps with me nights, I can't do much. . . . But I shall do it at last" (Annie Fields).

While Harriet was in Cincinnati, her sixth child, a particular favorite of hers, died of cholera at eighteen months. Her own spirit broke as she suffered from the same paralyzing depression as her father, and she had a gloomy view of her health. In a letter to her husband, she described the cholera plague raging in Cincinnati: "This week has been unusually fatal. Hearse drivers have hardly been allowed to unharness their horses, while furniture carts and other vehicles are often employed for the removal of the dead."

In spite of other family problems and her grief, her basic faith in the Lord was firm, though she had times of bewilderment. Her beautiful hymn "Still, Still with Thee" was written not long after her son died.

> *Still, still with Thee, when purple morning breaketh,*
> *When the bird waketh, and the shadows flee;*
> *Fairer than morning, lovelier than the daylight,*
> *Dawns the sweet consciousness, I am with Thee.*
>
> *So shall it be at last, in that bright morning,*
> *When the soul waketh, and life's shadows flee;*
> *O in that hour, fairer than daylight dawning,*
> *Shall rise the glorious thought, I am with Thee."*

When Calvin accepted a teaching job at Bowdoin College in Brunswick, Maine, Harriet was glad to leave Cincinnati where it was dangerous to be an abolitionist. Settled in her new home in 1851, she began writing *Uncle Tom's Cabin* in serial form for an abolitionist magazine, *National Era*. But she had interruptions. Various family members came to visit, and Harriet often used the kitchen table as her desk in an effort to find privacy.

Her sister Catharine saw that Harriet could not go on with her writing unless she had some freedom, so she spent one year in the Stowe home helping out. *Uncle Tom's Cabin* was published in forty issues of *National Era*, for which Harriet received $400.

She had conceived the basic plot during a Communion service emphasizing the conflict between good and evil. The following conversation took place with her friend Mrs. Howard:

"I did not write that book."

"What! You did not write *Uncle Tom?*"

"No, I only put down what I saw."

"But you have never been in the South, have you?"

"No, but it all came before me in visions, one after another, and I put them down in words." Later Harriet said, "I did not write it; God wrote it. I merely took His dictation."

Mrs. Howard said, "God inspires His children, and mighty works do still show forth . . . in those who are prepared. . . ."

As Mary said to the angel, "Behold the handmaid of the Lord; be it unto me according to thy word" (Luke 1:38).

Uncle Tom's Cabin was published as a book in 1852 and in a few days had sold 10,000 copies. Harriet became famous overnight. This powerful, controversial antislavery book had an amazing reception for a novel and took the world by storm. It was a runaway bestseller with sales in the millions. There were many translations. It is said that some Russians freed their serfs out of pity when they read the book.

In the story a slave, Uncle Tom, is sold by the Shelbys to the St. Clare family, separating him from his wife and child—one of the chief evils of slavery. He never sees his family or cabin again. However, Tom is well treated by both the Shelbys and St. Clares because they admire and trust his noble character.

When Tom is sold, he says, "I'm in the Lord's hands. The Lord, He'll help me. I know He will." Tom believed that the Lord is a loving, peaceful God. Stowe portrays Tom as what she thinks a Christian should be. When Tom was asked how he knew he was a Christian, he answered, "Felt Him in my soul, Mas'r—feel Him now!"

After the tragic death of little Eva St. Clare, Tom is sold to Simon Legree, a Northener from Vermont. Legree's mother is a pious, devoted Christian, but Simon himself is a monster wholly given over to evil. He runs a terribly brutal Southern plantation.

When Tom refuses to betray other slaves, Simon whips him to death. Before he dies as a martyr, Tom forgives everyone, even Simon. This event in *Uncle Tom's Cabin* reminds one of martyrs of the Christian faith who shine in the midnight of man's inhumanity to man.

A secondary plot tells of a couple, the Harrises, who make a dramatic escape by the Underground Railroad to Canada. The novel ends in a plea for the South to abolish slavery.

Unlike William Lloyd Garrison, who demanded immediate freedom for slaves, Harriet modestly hoped her book would help bring slavery to an eventual peaceful end. She played a major role in the antislavery struggle. However, her book increased hostility between the North and the South. Historians believe it was one of the factors leading to the Civil War, as Americans were stirred up about the plight of the slaves.

At the end of her preface to *Uncle Tom's Cabin* Harriet wrote:

The great cause of human liberty is in the hands of one of whom it is said:

> *"He shall not fail nor be discouraged*
> *Till He have set judgment in the earth,*
> *He shall deliver the needy when he crieth,*
> *The poor, and him that hath no helper.*
> *He shall redeem their soul from deceit and violence,*
> *And precious shall their blood be in His sight."*

Remembering that the North as well as the South long maintained this barbaric system of slavery, she wrote in her concluding remarks, "Both North and South have been guilty before God, and the Christian church has a heavy account to answer. Not by combining together to protect injustice and cruelty, and making a common capital of sin, is this Union to be saved, but by repentance, justice, and mercy . . . [for] injustice and cruelty shall bring on nations the wrath of Almighty God."

Although Harriet Beecher Stowe had visited a slave state, Kentucky, only once, her book presents a realistic account of America ten years before the Civil War. Her style is dramatic, with strong descriptive powers and touches of humor, and certainly at times is overly sentimental. No book up to this time had such a range of black characters. Harriet thought that the degradation of slavery had prevented African-Americans from developing their gifts in music, dancing, athletics, science, religion, kindliness, and warmth.

Stowe was loved in the North. Frederick Douglass (1817-1895) gave *Uncle Tom's Cabin* great praise. He said the book was "plainly marked by the hand of God," although he felt Uncle Tom was too subservient. Born a slave himself, Douglass was a leading spokesman for African-Americans. After escaping to freedom, he devoted his life to the abolition of slavery and the fight against segregation. His home was a station on the Underground Railroad. He complained to Harriet that many Northern churches did not take a stand against slavery.

The South received *Uncle Tom's Cabin* with outrage and invective. Southern writers turned out novels that bitterly attacked Harriet. This literature was often written from the viewpoint of benevolent slave owners and their even kinder wives.

All races have an innate desire for freedom. At the time many seemed blind to the irony of America proudly calling itself the land of the free in the face of rampant slavery. In the South people frequently appealed to the Bible to justify this evil.

The poet Longfellow commented about Harriet, "How she is shaking the world with her *Uncle Tom's Cabin.*" When Harriet met Lincoln during the darkest days of the Civil War, he said gently, "So you are the little woman who wrote the book that made this great war!" He also said, "If slavery is not wrong, nothing is wrong."

In 1863 President Lincoln issued a historic document, the Emancipation Proclamation that eventually led to the end of slavery. The document declared freedom for all slaves in all areas of the Confederacy still in rebellion against the North and also provided for the service of African-Americans in the Union Army. Later the Thirteenth Amendment ended slavery in all parts of the United States. Many black people went to Liberia to begin a new life there. In *Uncle Tom's Cabin* Harriet had written about African-Americans going to that country.

Harriet's book was widely read and praised in England. When the Stowes visited there in 1853, they were warmly welcomed by English abolitionists, especially William Wilberforce. Lord Shaftesbury called *Uncle Tom's Cabin* "that marvelous book." The Stowes dined with Thackery, Dickens, Kingsley, and Gladstone, and later with the Brownings in Italy. Harriet became a friend of George Eliot, and they kept up a correspondence for years.

In 1852 Charles Dickens wrote that he considered *Uncle Tom's Cabin* a noble work, with the gentlest, sweetest, and yet boldest writing. He also mentioned that her masterpiece was not free from the fault of overstrained conclusions and violent extremes. This observation is particularly humorous for those of us who love Dickens and read and reread his books, because his novels definitely share this weakness.

Uncle Tom's Cabin was made into a popular play as well as suffering various distorted dramatizations, often without the Stowes' permission. Harriet was world famous when she died at age eighty-five. In 1896 her collected writings were published in sixteen volumes. Her masterpiece *Uncle Tom's Cabin* is one of the most influential books ever written.

BIBLIOGRAPHY

Fields, Annie. *Life and Letters of Harriet Beecher Stowe*. Detroit: Gale Research Co., 1970.

Gossett, Thomas F. *Uncle Tom's Cabin and American Culture*. Dallas: Southern Methodist University Press, 1985.

RECOMMENDED READING

Uncle Tom's Cabin, or Life Among the Lowly

EDITH WHARTON

1862-1937

My ruling passions:
Justice-order, Dogs, Books, Flowers, Architecture, Travel and
A good joke—perhaps that should have come first.

Edith Wharton

After reading Edith Wharton's first novel, *The Valley of Decision*, Henry James wrote her an admonishing letter: "Do New York! The first-hand account is precious." Although James had not yet met her, he wanted her to give up foreign and historical writing and be "tethered in native pastures." It was the wisest literary advice she ever received and resulted in her finest psychological novels—about the cream of society who based their lives on amusement.

At James's urging Wharton's next powerful novel, *The House of Mirth,* has a New York setting and is now considered among the finest American novels of manners. It describes "a world of opulence where those of enormous fortunes want to show off their wealth." This book was a stunning success and soon became a bestseller, earning a fortune that supported Edith and her husband, Teddy. She wrote about what she had experienced, and she well understood the social changes she described.

Edith Newbold Jones was the last child born into a socially prominent and wealthy family in New York City. Her mother was only interested in a superficial social life, but her loving, kind father taught her to read the classics and to delight in art galleries, gardens, and classical ruins. The Jones family lived for six years in Paris, Florence, Rome, and Germany. Encouraged by her father from childhood, Edith struggled to be creative, imaginative, and productive in a world alien to her talents. Unconsciously, she was absorbing all she saw, and her love for beauty found expression in writing.

The Jones family returned to New York in 1872 when Edith was ten. The shock of leaving Europe was acute for her. With little guidance from adults, in her loneliness she found her mentors in books and contentment in reading and writing. She said, " I cannot remember a time when I did not want to make up stories." Gradually her family became alarmed by her growing shyness and passion for learning. At seventeen she made her New York debut, forced into the social life by her mother. She was told, "Women do not write."

With the death of her father in Cannes, France, Edith lost the companion who had taken her to art galleries, churches, theaters, and who had been with her in all the important places of her life. Back in New York, she resentfully and stiffly resumed a superficial social life dominated by the tastes of her mother.

In 1885 she married Edward (Teddy) Wharton, who was thirteen years older. He had no profession and lived on an allowance from his parents. She lacked basic information about sex and was ill-prepared for this marriage. They set up housekeeping in Newport, Rhode Island— "This ultra-frivolous milieu"—and led a full social life, traveling yearly to Europe.

Teddy's interest was sports. His pathetically shallow mind gave him little understanding of Edith's intellectual abilities and her serious resolution to become a writer. They were thoroughly mismatched and often very unhappy. However, in the early years Teddy was dedicated to Edith's every wish.

Teddy was a manic-depressive right out of Edith's later writing. She wrote of the sadness of a husband and wife not bound by common passions. One partner, a social butterfly (Teddy), lived idly on allowances, without responsibility or much conscience; the other partner (Edith) was serious about writing, industrious, and determined to get things done. The Whartons had no children.

Edith loved gardens, flowers, architecture, and beautiful homes. She was handsome and always exquisitely dressed, waited on by a variety of servants. A perfectionist and a fiercely energetic person, she could be rude, demanding, and sarcastic. She was a snob, wanting aesthetic perfection in everything and everyone around her.

In 1889 her first poems were accepted for publication. As her fame grew, she acquired many friends and was an admirable hostess. She was difficult, but not mean, and knew exactly what she wanted. She was a marvelous friend to those she chose as friends.

In 1897, with the architect Ogden Codman, Edith wrote *The Decoration of Houses*. A classic book about how to house oneself in elegance, beauty, simplicity and practicality, it was an instant success. This subject absorbed Wharton all her life, as she continued to build large, handsome homes or redecorate them during her many moves in America and later in Europe.

She believed that the building of houses created order in people's lives. Beautiful gardens were an intricate part of each of her homes. Although a superb gardener herself, she merely gave the orders, and a team of gardeners did the work. When friends recalled her name, they remembered a garden perfect in beauty.

After periods of frantic activity, Wharton would collapse. At the completion of *The Decoration of Houses,* she was treated for depression. Above all, travel helped her over her spells of despondency, as she believed change of scenery was a good cure. At the turn of the century, she and her husband began to spend more time in Europe. She probably crossed the Atlantic between sixty and seventy times. Henry James called her "the pendulum woman."

In 1902 the Whartons moved to their huge, newly built mansion, the Mount, in Lenox, Massachusetts. Here she wrote from 7:30 A.M. until noon, while the many guests entertained themselves. She described her beautiful garden in her next book, *The House of Mirth* (1905). The title comes from Ecclesiastes 7:4: "The heart of fools is in the house of mirth."

The story tells of the handsome Lily Bart's downfall from New York high society and her sad death.

The novel opens in New York's Grand Central Station, suggesting the transient quality of Lily's homeless existence. She is on the way to an elegant house party in the luxurious Bellomont Mansion. With biting satire Wharton exposes the shallow values of the dull, idle rich and the effect on Lily. Lily was born into that world but exists on its fringes because she has no money. Her only hope is a good marriage. Wharton explores the greed, extravagance, and pettiness of moneyed American families, the ultra-fashionable dancing people. Edith lived in this world, knew its dehumanizing qualities, and understood how difficult it was to remain single and survive.

Valued like a decorative object only for her stunning beauty, Lily is incapable of serious and significant action. At the conclusion of the novel, she ends up in a cheap boarding house where she commits suicide.

In 1906 the Whartons spent several months in Paris and in England with Henry James, one of America's greatest authors. The three went on many motor trips together through the years, including a visit to the home of author George Sand at Nohaut. Edith wrote of James, "His friendship has been the pride and honor of my life." James had a fifty-year writing career and was an important theorist of the novel.

Henry James (1843-1916) was born in New York City into a wealthy, intellectual family. His brother, William James, was a well-known and influential philosopher with whom Gertrude Stein studied. Henry James never married and suggested that to be an artist, a person should be free of the obligations of family life. However, he had a wide circle of literary friends, such as Edith Wharton, Flaubert, Turgenev, and Emile Zola. James lived mainly in Europe and finally settled in England where he became a British subject.

Through James, who visited at the Mount in 1907, Edith met W. Morton Fullerton. Her marriage with Teddy had long become insupportable. Teddy's health grew worse and worse as he often collapsed into deep depression. He spent a great deal of Edith's money, embezzling some, and even kept a mistress.

Edith moved to France in 1907 and began an affair with Fullerton in 1908. The relationship ended in 1911 when she discovered that the handsome bisexual Fullerton was a trivial cad who had had many other affairs. She probably never entered into an extramarital relationship again because she knew it was unsatisfactory.

In 1911, while Edith was writing *Ethan Frome,* both Teddy and Henry James were deeply depressed. In this novella Wharton expresses her sense of being controlled by other people's illnesses. Presenting a grim side of rural life, the story takes place in western Massachusetts. It is a nightmarish triangle of characters—Ethan, his wife, Zeena, and Zeena's cousin Mattie, who comes to help on their poor farm.

Ethan hasn't the emotional strength to leave the little village of Starkfield and go to Florida because his wife is always sick. When Ethan falls in love with Mattie, his jealous wife insists that Mattie leave, although she has no place to go. A failed suicide attempt leaves Ethan and Mattie maimed and under the control of Zeena. Mattie is the new whiny invalid.

Disappointing sales of this American classic contributed to the necessity to sell the Mount. With this loss, Edith's separation from Teddy became final. Many of her friends were divorced, and she wrote several stories about marital breakups, including *The Age of Innocence.* The idea of divorce always troubled Edith, but at last, in 1913, she and Teddy legally ended their marriage. This event also marked her estrangement from America. She began to associate the United States with materialism and greed. She saw France as having finer values, and she never regretted her transplantation to Europe.

She became friends with the great art critic Bernard Berenson and his wife, Mary, in Paris. Berenson had become a legend through his writings, and he understood "the art of looking." Edith herself as a writer saw the world as a series of pictures. Her friendship with Berenson lasted over thirty years and was one of spiritual intimacy and fraternal affection. They both had a passion for beauty.

In August 1913 Edith and Berenson toured Germany in her motor car. She always traveled with a maid, a chauffeur, and her agent, and they stopped often for picnics and brisk walks. Edith was a keen observer and wrote many articles about her motor trips, especially those in Italy and France. Several of her short stories and travel books are about Italian villas and gardens.

Edith Wharton was a fiercely energetic person, but frequently illness or a nervous breakdown brought her restless activities to a halt. She suffered strong mood swings and depression, especially after writing a book. Berenson observed that when things did not suit her, she was often on the verge of hysterics. But motor trips with Berenson, Henry James, and her cousin Walter Berry were always helpful. She loved good conversation with intellectuals.

Berenson thought Wharton's luxurious, cushioned way of life prevented her from experiencing reality. She was used to all the comforts of the very rich. Like Berenson, she often wrote in bed and spent hours reading there too. She was fussy about hotels, food, and waiters, frequently sending back every dish.

During the First World War, called "the Great War," Edith plunged into charity work because she was passionately committed to the French cause. With her organizational talents and the help of her friend Elisina Tyler, she opened three large houses in Paris for refugees and started an employment agency to help them find work. In the first year work was found for 3,400 refugees. She also began a convalescent home for sick women and children and started a lace-making school for the older girls. Often using her own money, she assisted soldiers who had contracted tuberculosis in the trenches.

With her friend and cousin Walter Berry she fearlessly visited the front lines, carrying supplies to devastated regions. She saw and heard of terrible atrocities and learned to hate the Germans. For her charities she raised large sums of money, especially in the States, and continually urged America to enter the war. Later she was appointed a chevalier of France's Legion of Honor in recognition of her remarkable war work.

After the war, having been very generous with her money, Edith began to have financial worries. She had inherited money and earned a great deal more, but she had given away a lot to the war effort.

She was a disciplined writer with an encyclopedic mind and rigid control, a shrewd businesswoman, and head of a complicated household of servants. Many of her employees had been with her for a long time and really were like family. They took good care of her and forgave her for her foibles and demanding ways. They also cared for her dogs that she loved so fanatically. When faithful servants died, she was devastated. However, the old roles of "servants and mistresses" had become a thing of the past.

In 1919 Edith, who preferred the country to the city, moved ten miles outside of Paris where she restored the splendid country home and gardens of Pavillon Colombe. Here as the perennial hostess, she received guests and had tranquillity for writing.

It was in this peaceful retreat that she wrote *The Age of Innocence* with the literary assistance of Walter Berry, who was a close friend of French novelist Marcel Proust. Berry often helped her with her writing and traveled widely with her, encouraging her in her many struggles.

In *The Age of Innocence* Wharton sought to describe the atmosphere of New York's high society of her youth. The story concerns the passion of Newland Archer for the beautiful Countess Ellen Olenska. Ellen has escaped Europe to seek refuge among her relatives because of a disastrous marriage to a Polish count.

Archer is engaged to marry wealthy Mary Wellard, who is good though unimaginative. In spite of his love for Ellen, he is unable to break free from convention. Ellen Olenska returns to Paris, and the rest of Archer's life is dull and unfulfilling. Here Edith Wharton is dealing with the problem and shame of divorce, which she too had experienced.

Edith Wharton received the Pulitzer Prize for *The Age of Innocence* in 1921. In 1923 she was the first woman to receive an honorary Doctorate of Letters from Yale. It occasioned her last trip to America.

The rise of Mussolini to power in 1922, Hitler in 1933, and Stalin in Russia caused Edith great concern. Even more personally for her, the

American financial crash in 1929 increased her worry over money. To earn more income she maintained a constant literary output.

She wrote her autobiography, *A Backward Glance,* in 1933. These memoirs describe her escape from the conventional world of her New York childhood into a self-created world where she could be herself and write. As a feminist she insisted that women mattered as much as men, but she believed that life for the American woman was a prison from which there was no escape. In her autobiography, as in life, she maintained her privacy. She openly laughed but would never show her grief. The review of *A Backward Glance* in the *Times* said, "She has written one of her most delightful books . . . evoking a vanished world and investing it with body and warmth and a peculiar leisured and gracious charm."

Edith continued traveling with friends, especially in Italy, where she wrote "Roman Fever," her best short story with an Italian setting. This wonderful tale, written at the height of her powers, recalls the experience of American travelers to Italy while portraying one of Wharton's passionate triangular relationships. She loved Roman rituals and the pageantry of the church and theater, but one senses a spiritual emptiness throughout her work. It is amazing what image-bearers of the Creator God are able to accomplish even when they do not acknowledge Him.

In her French retreat, however, she was moving back into the past emotionally and gradually lost touch with the modern world as a subject for fiction. After a stroke in 1935, she grew increasingly feeble but began *The Buccaneers,* a novel she never completed. Meanwhile, her short story "The Old Maid," later made into a movie, began a successful Broadway run, and there was also a dramatization of *Ethan Frome.* At seventy-five Wharton suffered another stroke, a fatal one, in her exquisite home, Pavillon Colombe. She had remarked, "It is good to grow old—as well as die—in beauty." She was buried at Versailles close to Walter Berry, who had helped her in her writing all through his life. What an extraordinary woman—productive to the end.

BIBLIOGRAPHY

Dwight, Eleanor. *Edith Wharton: An Extraordinary Life*. New York: Harry N. Abrams Inc., Publisher, 1994.

RECOMMENDED READING

The House of Mirth
Ethan Frome
The Age of Innocence
A Backward Glance
"Roman Fever"
"The Old Maid"

ABOUT THE AUTHORS

Jane Stuart Smith graduated with honors in liberal arts from Stuart Hall and Hollins College in Virginia. She studied further at the Juilliard School of Music in New York and the Tanglewood Festival School of Music in Massachusetts. Her chief voice teacher was Maestro Ettore Verna. As a dramatic soprano, Miss Smith has sung in major opera houses in Europe and America. At present she lives in Switzerland where she is a member and the International Secretary of L'Abri Fellowship. She lectures on art, literature, and music. In her many years in Huemoz, she has organized and participated in numerous art and musical festivals and given concerts in the United States, Canada, and Europe with the L'Abri Ensemble.

Betty Carlson has a B. A. degree from Grinnell College, an M.S. from Oregon State University, and has also studied at the Conservatory of Music in Lausanne, Switzerland. Among the various books she has written are *The Unhurried Chase, A New Song from L'Abri, No One's Perfect*, and *Reflections from a Small Chalet*. She is a volunteer helper at L'Abri Fellowship.

The authors have written five books together: *A Surprise for Bellevue, The Gift of Music, Favorite Women Hymn Writers, Favorite Men Hymn Writers*, and *Thoughts on Art, Literature, and Humor*.

Select Bibliography

Bartlett, John. *Familiar Quotations*. Boston: Little, Brown and Company, 1941.

Lane, Maggie. *Literary Daughters*. London: Robert Hale, 1989.

Smith, Jane Stuart and Betty Carlson. *Thoughts on Art, Literature, and Humor*. Huemoz, Switzerland: Le Petit Muveran Publishers, 1987.

Untermeyer, Louis. *A Treasury of Great Poems*. New York: Simon and Schuster, 1942.

_____. *Makers of the Modern World*. New York: Simon and Schuster, 1966.

Webster's New World Companion to English and American Literature. London: World Publishing Company, 1973.

The World Book Encyclopedia. Chicago: World Book, Inc., A. Scott Fetzer Company, 1994.

INDEX